Amanda has attended our training events for several years. Her ability ~~...~~
nd her ability to implement what she has learned put her in a rare group of leaders."

—Marc Accetta
Director of International Training, marcaccettaseminars.com

"The transformation Amanda has gone through in the last several years is truly
'mazing. When we first met, she was an elementary school teacher with no clue about
'usiness or network marketing. Her passion, drive for success, and heart for others in
'er work-from-home career is second to none. After witnessing her first day of business,
vhere she went 0-19, I never thought she'd be having the success she's enjoying today."

—Jeremiah Dew
Owner, Dew Productions, LLC (itsJDew.com)

"I met Amanda after the tragic suicide death of her son. I am impressed with her
'assion and drive to want to help people make a difference in whatever they attempt
' accomplish in life."

—Clark Flatt
President, The Jason Foundation, Inc., jasonfoundation.com

"Amanda Meyer is a powerful force and a beacon of light at the same time! I have
'atched Amanda deal with life's challenges in amazement and wonder many times
ver, as she draws on her amazing resolve to continue to help and impact others. If you
're being tested, if you feel as though you are on trial, or under fire, Amanda's story will
'elp you create your own testimony."

—Akil Huntley-Cooper
Network Marketing National Trainer & Million Dollar Earner

"We met Amanda four years ago at a company convention. She was bold and energetic as she approached us to introduce herself. We immediately related to one another because of our fitness career background, as we had both trained and prepped for fitness competitions. We knew right away that she does not shy away from hard work and commitment. She is proactive and strong-willed, which has gotten her far and will continue to be a major component of her success. We commend her for redirecting the pain and sadness that came from such an incredibly unfortunate and traumatic event in her life with the loss of her teenage son, into helping spread awareness and compassion to others who have experienced the same pain from suicide. She has always lit up any room she walks into, but now she has spread that light to the world."

—Brittany & Travis Jus
@TheHomeless_Millionaire

"I have known Amanda Meyer for over a decade, and I have admired her compassion as a mother and educator. She instinctively understands how to connect with people on their specific level and knows how to meet them where they are in their lives and businesses. Amanda is passionate about her family, friends, travel, and teaching others. She has taken the very difficult tragedy of losing her son, Logan, to remind others to make the most of every day, and she lives life to the fullest. Amanda is an amazing person with the personality to succeed and enjoys helping others to do the same."

—Laura Stanbr
Realtor/Broker/Real Estate Investor
Top 10 Individual Realtor for Real Estate Sale
Greenville, South Carolina

BREAKTHROUGH
SUCCESS
WITH AMANDA MEYER

ALSO FEATURING
OTHER TOP AUTHORS

© 2020 Success Publishing

Success Publishing, LLC
P.O. Box 703536
Dallas, Texas 75370 USA

questions@mattmorris.com

TABLE OF CONTENTS

CHAPTER 1

FINDING YOUR PURPOSE

By Amanda Meyer

I believe that there are three types of people. The first are the ones who go through life with a level of certainty, knowing their life's purpose and who they were destined to be; the second type spend the majority of their lives searching for their life's purpose and who they are destined to be; the third type are those who struggle throughout their lives, merely existing and without any desire to discover who they are destined to be.

I remember having that A-Ha moment at nine years of age and living in Florida. I recall it being a beautiful summer's evening. I looked up to the stars above and dreamed of becoming an astronaut. But there was an obstacle: I knew that one needed great intelligence to accomplish something like that, but I was a C student at best. I had battled with reading comprehension throughout my entire school-life. In some ways, I was fortunate that my parents never pressured me to aim at going to college. The only thing I really had was the desire to travel. As we lived so close to Miami, I decided to try to break into the modeling industry. For that, I didn't have to be "book smart," and I thought it would pay me enough to travel and see the world.

I was a typical teenager—I thought I knew everything, so the summer before my senior year, I decided to move out of my parent's house and get my own place. That meant I had to choose where I was going to live and how I was going to complete my last year of education. I was determined to figure out how to accomplish that, when the restaurant owners where I was working at the time invited me to live rent-free with them in their two-bedroom apartment. But there were two conditions: the first was that I complete my senior year and graduate on time; the second was that I had to be clean and tidy and buy my own groceries.

But after a few months of living with them, I thought it best to find work elsewhere. The $4.25 an hour they were paying me to be a hostess was no longer enough to live on, especially now that I was "on my own." I needed more than just an hourly wage and was lucky enough to find a waitressing job at a sports bar in the next town. I had to hustle for every dollar, but I knew that the harder I worked, the more money I would make. Then came a night when one of the bartenders didn't show up for their shift. This was my opportunity; "Amanda, we need you behind the bar!" the manager yelled at me. Well, bartending paid better than waitressing, but I'd never done it before. I didn't know then what I soon learned; in the words of Richard Branson, "If somebody offers you an amazing opportunity, but you are not sure if you can do it, say yes—then learn how to do it later."

My schedule at this point was bartending until 2 a.m., getting home by 3:30 a.m., and then getting up for school at 6:30 a.m. I was sleep-deprived and pretty much slept through my entire senior year. I did only the bare minimum necessary to graduate. By that time, I was beyond mentally and physically exhausted, but was determined to graduate on time because I had given my word to the people who had given me a shot and a free place to live. I thought I owed it to myself as well. What would it have said about my integrity if I hadn't followed through with what I had said I was going to do? It would have been crazy to quit just at the point when, after eleven years of what I considered the agonizing pain of attending school, I was about to graduate—which I did in the spring of 1995. Having, at last, managed to achieve what I set out to do, I felt a huge sense of accomplishment. However, now that I was an adult in the real world, I began questioning what my purpose in life was.

was twenty-four when I married my first husband, gave up on my dreams of traveling the world, and moved to Texas. At twenty-six, I gave birth to our son, Logan. I found myself in a tumultuous and unhealthy marriage, where we did nothing but argue. We were great parents to Logan, but we were not great together, so we called it quits on our marriage. I felt a huge sense of failure, being a single parent aged twenty-seven. I had no college degree, was bartending until 4 a.m., pawning my child off on anyone who would watch him while I worked, because I had no support system, as my family lived on the East Coast. My life had no direction. I felt lost, defeated, and broken. I felt that I needed some time to re-evaluate my life and set myself some goals, but instead, I jumped into another marriage one year later.

At the start of my second marriage, my husband was good to me, and, even more importantly, he was good to my son. He was in the military, so my son and I made the move to Georgia to be with him. At twenty-nine, I went through a heartbreaking miscarriage, but, one year later, I gave birth to our beautiful daughter, Mackenzie. Being a new mom again was exhausting, but I finally decided to re-enter education and study for a teaching degree. Parenting two phenomenal kids, being a military spouse, working as a bartender, and going to school certainly put strain on our marriage. Somewhere along the way, we stopped respecting one another. I certainly didn't want another divorce, but I eventually found out that my spouse had been cheating on me for over a year. I found myself in another failed marriage. I knew I had to figure out how I was going to survive life sucker-punching me once again, but how was I going to juggle being a single parent, working, and continuing my education all at the same time? I learned that when your back is up against the wall, you go into fight or flight mode.

I realized that I could accomplish anything with drive, determination, and a clear plan of action. I refused to fail or feel like a failure ever again. I ended my first semester of school with three A's, and, for the first time in my entire thirty-two years, I felt smart. All I had needed was a little bit of belief in myself that I was capable of achieving my dreams, and I firmly believe that with belief in ourselves, we can all become who we want to become.

Over the next few years, the kids and I moved to South Carolina, where completed my degree and graduated—with honors. During that time, I me the love of my life. With two failed marriages on my track record, I felt a b undeserving of any chance at happiness, but he restored my faith in marriag on many levels. Finally, things seemed to be going my way: I was married to wonderful man. I fell in love with his three older children, and our two familie became one. I started my teaching career at the school my children attended, an I was finally feeling as though everything was coming together at last. Then, thre years into teaching, I found myself working sixty-hour weeks while being bullie by the administration. I was burned out, and I did not like myself anymore, a a parent or wife; I realized that something had to change. I knew if I didn't a something different, I wouldn't *have* anything different. Around this time, a frien introduced me to network marketing. It was not something I thought I woul end up doing, especially after working so hard to get my degree, but I decided t step out of my comfort zone. Through personal growth and development, visior and the desire to help others, I was able to retire from the teaching professio twenty-five years early and pursue the life I know I was destined to live. I neede to immerse myself in a culture of personal growth and development. I realize my purpose in life was to be an educator, but not just in a classroom setting. don't believe it's quitting to walk away from something that isn't serving you wel whether it be a failing relationship or a career you have put your blood, sweat, an tears into. To do so is being smart enough to know when someone or somethin is preventing you from growing and fulfilling your life's purpose.

By the time 2019 came around, I truly felt I had it all: the perfect family, a positiv set of friends, money from my passion, and not a paycheck. I was finally travelin the world for a living as I had always dreamed of doing. But it's frightening ho quickly life can humble you. My husband and I were in Netherlands, enjoyin the sights and time together until, one evening, I was awakened by a phone call. was every parent's worst nightmare: my son, Logan, who was sixteen at the tim as on the train tracks wanting to end his life. Everything suddenly screeched to a alt. There I was, sitting halfway across the world, feeling helpless and completely evastated. Guilt at my failure as a parent immediately consumed my entire being. Where had I gone wrong? What could I have done differently? A thousand and ne questions and thoughts fluttered through my head, all paralyzing my body ut leading to one simple answer . . . nothing.

ooking back now, I feel that a part of me died that day, but what I have come ɔ realize through my tragedy is that people who decide to take their own lives on't really want to end it all, they just lose their purpose. Somewhere, somehow, ιy son felt as if he had no purpose in life. Since losing Logan, I have made it ιy life's mission to help others find their purpose in life. I had to discover mine ll over again, and now I hope to inspire readers across the globe to step out of ιeir comfort zone and into the life they were designed and destined to live. The hoices we make in life lead us down the path that we are supposed to be on. It is milar to the butterfly effect: if you change one minor detail in your life, it will hange everything in your past and your future, so that wherever you find yourself t any point in life, it's where you are supposed to be. I live with no regrets, and am proud to say that I am still happily married to the love of my life for eleven ears and we enjoy a healthy relationship. Together, we are learning to navigate fe's ups and downs and heal as a family. My purpose in life is to travel the world nd change lives. I had no idea that it would take the sum of all my failures and :iumphs to figure that out. My son did not die in vain. He may have felt as if he ad no purpose, but maybe, it was only meant for him to have sixteen loving years f existence to make his imprint on the world.

Whatever life throws at you, you have to keep your feet moving—because it's not ιst about finding your purpose, it's about learning and enjoying the journey of :rowth along the way.

BIOGRAPHY

Amanda Meyer is a military spouse, mother of five children, and a fitne
competitor. With a bachelor's degree in Elementary Education, Amanda has taugh
writing to a wide range of age groups. Amanda has become a transformation;
leader within the network marketing industry, helping others achieve their goa
and dreams. After losing her sixteen-year-old son to suicide in 2019, Amanda's li
mission has been to travel around the world, helping others discover their purpos
in life. As a national motivational speaker, Amanda teaches and inspires others t
achieve success by stepping out of their comfort zone and into a life they wer
designed to live.

Amanda Meyer's contact details are available at https://linktr.ee/amandameyer202

CHAPTER 2

HOW TO DEAL WITH AN UNSUPPORTIVE SPOUSE IN BUSINESS

By Matt Morris

In the process of leading hundreds of thousands of entrepreneurs and salespeople over my twenty-five-year career, I've witnessed that relationship turmoil is one of the single biggest killers to success in business.

Nothing saps your energy or drains your spirit more than disharmony in the household.

Before we dive in, I want to make it clear . . . I'm no relationship Goo-Roo.

I'm divorced, so taking relationship advice from me might be a bit like learning how to get six-pack abs from a sumo wrestler.

So, while I'm no relationship expert, I am an expert in human nature. I've coached thousands of entrepreneurs over my career, and relationship disharmony that impacts negatively on business development is one situation that I've been able to coach many others through successfully.

Many of you reading this may not have this issue or may not even be in a relationship, but you must read this anyway, because, on your journey to leadership, this WILL undoubtedly be an issue for some of the people you lead.

My training here is assuming you're in a committed relationship, either married or headed in that direction.

7 WAYS TO OVERCOME AN UNSUPPORTIVE SPOUSE IN BUSINESS:

#1 Don't push

Are you pressuring and pushing your spouse to be as excited about your business as you are?

I know your first instinct is to say, "No, of course not."

But, if I were to ask your spouse if they're feeling pressured, what would they say?

If you suspect there is even a slight hint of this, I'd recommend you ask them and get their perspective on things. If you want them to understand your dreams and desires in business, then I suggest you follow the sage wisdom of Dr. Stephen Covey: *"Seek first to understand, then to be understood."*

The more you push, the more likely it is that you'll create conflict. Some people aren't wired for entrepreneurship or, at least, don't believe they are because of their beliefs. Instead of pressuring them to be excited, you should be you and let them be them.

If you want your spouse to support your dreams and desires, you first must try to understand their dreams and desires and make sure you support them, even though it might be difficult at times to fully understand each other's goals.

#2 If you want support, give support

How exactly are you giving support in the ways that your spouse wants the most?

Notice, I said, "in the ways that your spouse wants."

You may be providing money, a home, doing the cooking, and cleaning. Those may be important for you, but, in many cases, spouses aren't supportive because they don't feel supported in the ways that matter most to them.

How can you BE the example for support that you want to be? The answer may not be obvious to you, so you may need to dig in, ask, and work on resolving that question until you find the answer.

To sum it up, you must be the example.

3 Neutralize the threat

In many cases, an unsupportive spouse is unsupportive because they feel as though your business is a threat to the relationship. They may feel that you consider your business a bigger priority than the relationship and that your business is pulling you away from them.

You need to understand that this threat may not be vocalized because your spouse doesn't want to appear insecure or controlling. However, the reason they are not supportive could be because of their underlying fear and insecurity about the relationship.

For many entrepreneurs, this is hard to understand: in your mind, you're "doing the business for them" or for the family, and you've told them that. However, you must realize that even though that might be true for you, and even though you've told them that time and time again, they aren't feeling it.

So, how do you get them to feel it? Keep reading . . .

4 Honor them

Find ways to admire and acknowledge what you honor and respect about your spouse.

Whether we want to admit it or not, we all have a desire to be respected. If your spouse feels as though you're respecting your business or your business partners more than them, it will drive a wedge between the two of you.

If you want to be supported and honored as an entrepreneur, support and honor your spouse and other family members from whom you want support.

5 Appreciate them.

On a daily, yes, DAILY basis, take steps to ensure that your spouse feels genuinely appreciated. Of course, it's great to tell them, but folks generally see better than they hear, so make it a regular practice to write little letters or notes of appreciation for them. Even if it's just a sticky note, it shows that you care and make them feel appreciated and loved.

When you're out working on your business, take a few minutes to send them a text message appreciating and acknowledging them. I've seen relationships transform through the simple act of an appreciative text or sticky note sent every single day.

If you feel as though you've tried everything, then try writing a text or note to send them every single day for the next thirty days and see what happens.

Reward the behaviors you want.

When your spouse shows any sign of support, go overboard in showing your appreciation for that support.

#6 Unconditional love

In our heart of hearts, what we all want is unconditional love—to be loved no matter what.

When your spouse is unsupportive, understand that it's likely because of their fears, their lack of feeling supported themselves, their lack of feeling honored, appreciated, or loved. So, show your love for them, no matter what.

If you want them to support you, whether you're winning or not, love them whether they're demonstrating love for you or not.

Act to ensure that your spouse understands that they are the most important thing in your life and show that you love them, no matter what.

#7 SUCCEED

I've seen hundreds of people go from unsupportive to being their spouses' biggest fans when they see their spouses winning.

There's an old story from Tom "Big Al" Schreiter that fits here . . .

A husband gets involved in network marketing. He's super-excited and has a dream of buying a new Cadillac. He cuts out a picture of a Cadillac and tapes to their bathroom mirror. But when he gets home that night from work and busy day of doing meetings, his unsupportive wife takes the picture down and uts it in the drawer.

But, undeterred, the husband tapes it back up on the mirror. Then, when e comes home the next night, again, it's in the drawer.

This process repeats every day for months.

Until one day, the husband comes home with a brand-new Cadillac, bought 'ith money earned from the profits of his new business.

The next day, when the husband comes home, taped to their bathroom airror is a picture of a mink coat!

Your spouse wants to see you win, but they might not believe it's possible.

So, do all the things necessary to win.

BIOGRAPHY

.uthor of the international bestseller, *The Unemployed Millionaire*, Matt Morris egan his career as a serial entrepreneur aged eighteen. Since then, he has generated ver $1.5 billion through his sales organizations, with a total of over one million ustomers worldwide. As a self-made millionaire and one of the top internet nd network marketing experts, he's been featured on international radio and :levision and spoken from platforms to audiences in over twenty-five countries round the world. And now, as the founder of Success Publishing, he co-authors 'ith leading experts from every walk of life.

Contact Information

Website: http://www.MattMorris.com

Company website: http://successpublishing.com/

CHAPTER 3

THE PERSON YOU COULD HAVE BEEN

By Steve Moreland

I f Fate's blood-stained cauldron has not found your life yet, she's hiding just over the horizon, waiting until you're at your most vulnerable. So if you're willing to listen to someone that knows about life's ash heap, I'll share the lessons I learned after I failed my Test. The lessons focus on our thinking. More specifically, about how thinking differently empowered me to thrive where most cannot imagine surviving. I promise not to waste your time with fluffy bullshit or rah-rah! Just the mental tools what worked, that brought me across a desert wilderness of 5,544 days.

May the following battle-tested advice return you from your seemingly impossible cauldron *"tested—and found not wanting."*

We Texans pride ourselves on our Code. Toughness is Rule #1. And it means *"no tears allowed."* See, our cult-like indoctrination begins the moment we are born. And the other Spartan rules include: *do only BIG things*, especially if others say it can't be done; *rub some dirt on it* because blood and scars prove your worth; and *Do Right*, even if the Lord God, himself, threatens you to do otherwise!

Brutal. Absolutely! But definitely the kind of folks you'd want coverin your back in a fight. It's a belief carved deep in our soul—that there simply is NC FREE LUNCH. It is a creed rooted in commitment and perseverance, summe up in one word. Grit!

The standard we have to carry begins early. At age twelve, I started *"earnin my worth."* My phone rang off the wall with grass-cutting jobs in the Texas inferno called summer because my dad drilled me to do what everyone else is afraid of, t deliver results beyond expectations. Just self-disciplined results! No excuses.

I went right to corporate America after graduating with academi scholarships – working for three Fortune 500 companies before I was 24. A twenty-five I was in charge of my own brokerage firm in Dallas. By thirty, I'd mad it to millionaire status, flew in private jets, brokered 9-figure deals from Europea castles, banked in numbered Swiss accounts, and spoke on international stage raising millions for venture capital deals.

Ballistic was my term for the vertical climb I experienced. Simultaneousl serving as vice president of offshore operations for a boutique hedge fund, CEC of a 58-office tax and wealth management firm, and co-principal of a SaaS startup I couldn't afford the luxury of sleep. And part of every month, I lived near m office in the banking district of Nassau, Bahamas, acting as the vice president c business development for a middle eastern banking syndicate.

Occasionally, I woke up at a place my then-wife and children called hom It was there that I slowed down enough to rub some of that Texas dirt on my han tremors from sleeping only on those overseas flights. I was stumbling forward jus to maintain the pace.

There was something wrong but I could not risk failing the mission. M Dad's standing orders were crystal: *"You can rest when you're dead!"* And this belie came from his creed that a man only earns a medal on his gravestone if he die "in combat."

Well, I failed to become a "lifer" in the Corps, so I determined tha I was going to achieve whatever most would call impossible. I believed in hi invincibility! And after eighteen years of his Marine-style bootcamp, I feared onl one thing, **"meeting the person I could have been!"**

o, when Fate's blood-stained hurricane came for me, I was Ready. Ready to
lindly march into Hell itself. But after the first few years, I felt more like the
ireek myth of Sisyphus who was sentenced to pushing a boulder up the mountain
very damn day and then waking up the next morning to find it at the bottom
gain. I remember thinking to myself, "Maybe God is *not* good" after feeling
oul-crushing agony for the first time. Real pain that made me wish I could just
ie and get it over.

I'll admit, all that invincibility crap did NOT work. And I'm painfully
mbarrassed to admit that I found myself wallowing in my self-pity after losing
bsolutely everything and feeling abandonment by all I loved. I had succumbed
o that state of a *victim*. And you know what, that Texas dirt did NOT fix the
ounds I'd caused my family for the undeserved trials and tribulations my bull-
eaded foolishness caused.

Though I was brought up with my dad's relentless Texan and Marine Corp
ode of conduct mixed with my mom's Christian beliefs, the devasting pain
aused me to question their beliefs. Sitting in the ash heap of my life like the
ible's character Job, I commenced to blaming God for not protecting us from
ne horror that imprisoned us. I begged and even prayed for an instant release of
nisery, even raising my fist in anger and shouting "You're *NOT* a good god!"

I just wanted that magical snap of a finger and everything to be like it used
o be. But genie-like fixes never happen, do they. Why? Because strength is *not*
orged in luxury and comfort. Medals do not get pinned to your chest for holding
ands and singing "Kum Ba Yah."

The struggle to endure real agony, to eat suffering, and know your pain so
ntimately that you name her has a purpose. You see, it took time for me to get
ver my self-entitlement in order to face my demons and do the most excruciating
ning I'd ever done. Realizing that I could not change the past or erase what my
nistakes had cost my family, I had to make a decision: either continue to blame
thers and wallow in self-pity or use the hell I was inside to forge a better version
f me!

In school, we're first taught the lesson that prepares us for the test. But, in life we face the Test first; later, we learn the Lesson.

The grade is what we become through it all. It's pass or fail. And yes, hell is when you meet that person you could have been. It means rising again and again within the blood-stained cauldron of Fate. Only this repeated discipline distinguishes the few from the many, the extraordinary from the ordinary. The worthy from the worthless.

But that person you could have been is only Hell if he or she stands better than you chose to become! **Hell, then, is meeting the *better* person you could have been.**

Like I promised in the beginning, what follows WILL take you through any hell. And you will arrive on the other side, *"tested – and found not wanting."*

Let's begin with a question: "Have you ever been really curious about something—to the point of obsession?"

Since I was a kid, I wanted to unravel this thing called thinking. I reasoned to myself that if I could only understand how the few we call "great" actually thought, I might be able to be like them and make the world a little bit better. Because, for the most part, they are human just like me. The only difference is that they *see things differently* in their minds.

Personal development "coaches" blather about managing our thinking. It is THE key, agreed. But it's not enough to know *what* to do. We've got to know *how* to do it. It's the subtle and often hidden difference between learning science without the art of knowing how it applies to real-world situations. Most of these "well-meaning" coaches deserve an "A" for science but an "F" in art. Never earning a medal from within Fate's blood-stained cauldron means their theories can get you to one destination – that chance to meet the person you could have been.

Here's an example of a coach with earned rank, Dr. Viktor Frankl, author of *Man's Search For Meaning*. Frankl didn't just survive six years of Nazi concentration camps, he changed the world forever with his discovery of how we create meaning through our imagination.

better thinking creates better doing. And better doing creates a better being.

Frankl forced me to think. I mean really think. And all of a sudden, what Professor Eli Goldratt wrote in *The Goal* became crystal clear. "If we continue to do what we have done, which is what everybody else is doing, we will continue to get the same *unsatisfactory* result." But I asked myself, isn't that what we do so very often - more of what everyone else has done and then expecting a different outcome?

We are what we've done, right? So, aren't our own actions - what we *do* - that creates who we *become*? In short, "doing creates being." So, who we are today - our being, is a product of our past doings? Becoming someone better can only happen by doing differently. And differently results from the seed of the thoughts in our imagination.

Because I wanted a different future – one that honored the sacred by making the world better, I could no longer afford to think like I used to, or like everyone else. Maybe you're brighter than me and already know this. But for me, this realization was the Eureka! And in that realization, I felt something deep inside like lightning.

If my prior thinking caused my current doings (my actions and habits that are known as my reality), **then why couldn't I change my future by changing the way I was thinking?**

Socrates (Greek philosopher 470 B.C.) taught a Secret passed through his student Plato to his student Aristotle (Greek philosopher 384 B.C.). Aristotle planted his Secret into the mind of a 13-year-old prince. This Secret method of thinking changed the ancient world.

At 16 years of age, the prince led his cavalry at the Battle of Chaeronea, decimating a supposedly unbeatable enemy. At 20 years of age, he became king of Greece, marched his army towards Persia, solved the riddle of the Gordian Knot, and destroyed any that opposed.

At 24, he captured the supposedly unconquerable city of Tyre. At 25, he became Pharaoh of Egypt and then returned to the desert near modern-day

Babylon to lead his 50,000-man army against a force exceeding 500,000 led by the Persian emperor Darius. Charging into the front line on his legendary black stallion Bucephalus, he achieved the impossible and became emperor of the known world.

By age 30, he had created the largest empire in history. Today, he's still studied in war colleges for his battlefield genius, ethical governance, and unrivaled valor.

The Secret thought? "Be as you wish to seem."

The Result? One *impossible* difficulty after another - CRUSHED!

His Name? Alexander

How is he remembered? Alexander—the Great!

In school, we're first taught the lesson that prepares us for the test. But, in life, we face the Test first; later, we learn the Lesson.

Here's my experience. The Lessons learned *after* the Test lead to better actions—which lead to becoming a better being, right? That means that tests uncover our weaknesses so that we can learn greater lessons. What and who we become through the Tests reflects our grade in life.

If we're honest, we'll admit that we often create our own storms. And then we blame others when we must endure them. But if we use the agony, we find something called grit. Grit is commitment bathed in love to become better than we were the day before. It's a relentless dedication to rise—to become better, stronger, and wiser. It's a refusal to quit, even when we feel we can't get up again.

The question is, will we? Will we persist after the problems that were caused by our poor thinking – and the results that followed? Or will we just quit due to the fear of failing and the probability that life won't be easy?

Being *"tested and found not wanting"* means we'll certainly be scarred from one battle after another. But the scars reflect rank, defining how many times we returned to the cauldron instead of hiding and waiting to be rescued by the God that's testing us.

t may be cliché, but our very thinking sparks our every action. Put another way, ur doings, added together over time, construct our being - *what* and *who* we ecome.

Do we dishonor the Sacred, settling for what everybody else is doing and ontinuing to get their same *unsatisfactory* results?

Or do we ***think*** **better**, in order to ***do*** **better**, so that we could ***be*** **better**?

We become what we choose to be. This is the Secret. My gift to you, as aristotle long ago shared with Alexander, "be[come] as you wish to seem."

Now you know that Hell is NOT meeting the person you could have been.

Hell is meeting the *better* person you could have been.

BIOGRAPHY

A native Texan, Steve Moreland is known for two things. Dedicated practice. And success. Success equates to one's level of practice. So he really does only one thing. His Rubicon system teaches how to perform the common under uncommon onditions.

Motivated by the Latin creed FORTES FORTUNA ADIUVAT – "Fortune favors he brave," his mission is to deliberately cause affirmative outcomes that would not have occurred otherwise.

Connect with Steve via LinkTree: https://linktr.ee/steve_moreland

CHAPTER 4

THE MAGIC OF TIME

By Arjan Scholten

Time is life's great enigma. What is more mysterious than time? But what exactly is it, and what does it mean to us, as humans? And, perhaps most importantly, how does it work? In the course of my life, I've spent a lot of time thinking about time—and I believe that many of us are driven from time to time to ponder about the puzzle that time, as we know it, presents to us. And now, I'd like to invite you to spend a little time with me.

I was born in the Netherlands, and, as a young boy, suffered from a disease called asthma. It was challenging for a child to live with the disease. Although, in time, the disease would prove to be both a burden and a blessing in my life. When I was in my first year at primary school, I spent more time either at home or in the hospital because of the asthma. That was also the year that my parents got divorced. Because of the illness, I was made to repeat that first year of school, to make up for the time I had lost. You can imagine how I felt; it was a tough time, and it was difficult to connect with my classmates. I remember thinking that doing the same year over again at school meant that I would lose a year of my life. It's generally true that when you're young, you want to grow up fast. You want to go to bed late and do all the things that grown-ups are doing. Time never seems to go fast enough for you. Or at least, that's how it feels.

Over the next few years, my asthma became a real issue. I was 10, and m
parents decided that it really needed to be dealt with. So, they started to searc
for a healthier environment for me to live in, hoping that things would improv
and I would learn to live with my asthma. They came up with two options: On
was an asthma center based in Switzerland, the second was another clinic locate
in the Netherlands. That's how I ended up staying for 15 months in the clinic i
the Netherlands, far away from my parents, family, friends, or anyone familia
I felt lost and often wondered how the time spent in the clinic would benef
me. But, at the same time, I began to realize that maybe I should look at th
experience differently. Like it or not, the one thing that never changes for all c
us, human beings, is the fact that you live by yourself and, therefore, experienc
life by yourself. This was an incredible insight for me. At that young age, I learne
that I alone was responsible for connecting with people, forming my opinion
and living my life in a way that made sense to me. Some people might call this
kind of freedom. It was undoubtedly true that the idea of the constraints of tim
took on a completely different meaning for me than previously. I realized tha
there is no such thing as a time constraint because it's only a matter of what yo
believe. How you spend your time and what you do during the time you spend i
this world is entirely up to you. Based on my experience, my advice is to spend
wisely, for time is not coming back.

And so that is what I tried to do. I became the master of my own plar
not an organized plan, but one that unfolded based on life experiences. I finishe
attending MAVO secondary school in the Netherlands at the age of 17, an
wondered: What do I do now? Again, time became an issue for me. It was expecte
that, like most kids, I would find a course of study, go to college, and eventuall
get a master's degree in some field. But was that really what I wanted for mysel
I mean, what did I know of life? It goes by so fast and, besides, I had questior
about what kind of life choices I should make. It seemed crazy to be expected t
make choices about the right educational path to take. I thought that it might b
a good idea for me to take some time to find out who I was as a person.

But could I actually do that? My mind was full of what-ifs. You probab
know that feeling when your emotions seem to take over, and your good judgmer
becomes clouded. I felt so strongly that I needed more time to get to know me
So, I decided to leave my comfort zone and seek adventure! I still think it's real

nportant to find out who you are and how you tick, and only then make the big ecisions that will affect the rest of your life. So, at 17, I decided that, since life 'as happening all around me, I should do what I believed was going to be good r me!

I chose to find myself, to get familiar with the real Arjan and find out what e's about, before making any of those big choices. Up to that point, my life had een dictated by my upbringing, my disease, and a somewhat limited view of the orld. But my thoughts eventually led me to take a great leap forward into the nknown and embark on a big adventure: I decided to go abroad and live for a ear in the United States, where I would attend high school. That would give me chance to see how well I could manage and learn more about myself. It was a ary thought but, at the same time, full of promise and with the potential to be ery rewarding. You could say that I took a whole year out to study myself, Arjan cholten. What a great decision that was! By taking that time out, I learned so uch about life and myself. I'd say that it saved me years of struggling to find my urpose in life, and gave me time to shape my own beliefs and goals that I could and by. My life plan began to emerge—or, at least, I felt that I had an idea that, acted upon, could become a life plan.

At last, it seemed that my mission in life was clear. Best of all was the ealization that I had the whole of my life to make it happen. What a gift, and hat a time saver! Unlike many other people, who go through life, not knowing hat to do, when they're older, are left saying: "God, I wish I'd done so-and-so, ut now I'm too old, and there's no time left to live my dreams." Not for me!

After spending a year in the US, I returned to the Netherlands, a reborn oung man of 18. During my time away, I'd discovered that I had skills and ecided that I would use education to help me master them. I went to college and ventually earned myself a bachelor's degree in commerce.

I started working and became a CRM expert—that's Customer Relations Management. I believe that everything in life, whether it's to do with business or our personal life, is about the dialogue we have with one another. We, humans, ommunicate with each other all the time. That's how we relate to people—by iving time to each other. Back then, I felt strong and worked hard on the goals d set for myself, but, unfortunately, I forgot my health and the fact that I have sthma. I was working hard and playing hard and generally enjoying life. But, while doing that, I forgot that my system, my body, needed proper care and that my life-work balance needed to be in sync. I needed to establish healthier eating habits and exercise more often. Things came to a standstill when I was 32 and was hospitalized with severe lung problems. Before I knew it, I found myself in intensive care, multiple tubes going in and out of my body, and fighting to survive.

The doctor told me, when I came in, the condition of my lungs was like that of an 80-year-old. In other words, like those of someone who had not taken their health seriously at all.

I am very fortunate to be alive today. After spending three weeks in the hospital, I was finally released and able to go home. But, what a time I had at the hospital! When I was conscious and transferred from the intensive care unit to normal medical care, I had a lot of time to think. I lay awake for hours in bed, my life flashing before my eyes, as I realized that this might be it—my life could be over. I could have died right there and then: A young man who died at 32 due to a severe asthma attack. What a way to go! That was also the moment that I finally understood the wisdom of "health before wealth."

That was a hard lesson for me to learn and comprehend. It took me another six months of being at home to come to my senses. My pride became anger, then fear, and finally gratitude, gratitude for life, for just simply being around and hopefully, living happily ever after. So, once again, I made a life plan.

That plan contained everything. I'd learned from my experiences and the reason why I made the decision to enjoy life, to make the best of the time I have. Now, I make it my mission to inspire and help people by giving them—time:

- Time as a gift.
- Time to listen.
- Time to explain.
- Time to learn.
- Time to experience life.
- Time to feel.
- Time to express themselves.
- Time to love.

That's what I have learned: Time is magic. Scientifically speaking, you can say that a day has 24 hours, a week has 168 hours, and a year lasts for 365 days, which accounts for 8,768 hours. The United Nations estimate of the global average life expectancy in 2019 was 72.6 years; if we round it up—73 x 8,768—that quals 641 thousand hours. What do you mean, you don't have time? You have ll the time in the world! But that isn't all: Our experience of time is governed y our perception of time. As we grow up, our view of the world and, thus, our erception of time changes. Isn't it a true blessing and gift that time is so amazing? .nd it can be spent in any way we choose. But just bear in mind that once spent, 1at time won't come back—so my advice is to spend it wisely.

We forget that time is just an instrument, and that our lives and our time ccupy only a short period from a universal point of view. We humans feel, love, nd experience all sorts of other emotions. And that is a good thing. That makes .s special. So, be proud of yourself, and don't worry about the choices you've 1ade or are going to make. Time is experience, so experience it. I believe that veryone has their own life journey and that the most important thing is to make count.

Of course, people live and die, so why not make life a great journey? Take .me to think about what you want your life to be about. How would you like to e remembered? What will be your legacy? Remember, your life is over before you now it. But, as long you're here, enjoy it and make the best of the time you've een given. I wish you all the best. May this chapter serve you as time well spent.

BIOGRAPHY

.rjan Scholten is a CRM expert whose passion is to help people and businesses, ducating them about how processes can work in their favor. He's a big fan of ersonal development and learning how to have more fun in the workplace, and fe in general. His mission is to inspire people and help them live life to their .ll potential. He believes that, no matter what your past, you can move forward nd live your dream, simply by working passionately towards achieving it. Arjan's 1otto is: Live your life and make it happen.

Contact Information

acebook: https://www.facebook.com/ArjanScholtenTime
nstagram: https://www.instagram.com/arjanscholten71/

CHAPTER 5

GOING AGAINST THE GRAIN

By Ben Dahl

I still remember looking at that number, thinking, "I can't afford this." The $2,000 was more than I had in my bank account, and it would be the first time I had spent that much on anything. There I was, pacing around my disheveled room in a run-down college house in my torn sweatpants. It was an environment best suited for living life between beer cans and bottles of dip spit, but I was somewhere else in my mind. I believed I could do something more, and was about to make one of the biggest decisions of my life.

That is not to say that things were bad. I had a part-time job at a digital marketing agency in downtown Cincinnati. My boss had practically guaranteed me a position after graduation if I stuck around. I had earned membership in the most prestigious (and fun) fraternity on campus. I was dating an intelligent, kind, and beautiful girl. My social circle was so big I couldn't leave the house without seeing one of my friends. I rocked six-pack abs, held a position in the best business clubs on campus, maintained a 3.9 GPA in my honors program, competed in intramurals, and was hitting my stride in guitar practice.

Forgive me for sounding arrogant—life was good. You're probably thinking: "Dude, you had it made!" and I did, in a way. I had it made insofar as I could have

easily gone with the flow and achieved a relatively standard, white-collar qualit
of life without having to try.

So, what on God's green earth could possibly lead me to take all of m
money, including student loans, to buy a $2,000 online course on how to start
consulting business?

The simple answer is that "I wanted more."

Like so many of us, the path I was on at the time didn't reflect my dream

Do you ever feel that you were destined to do something great, somethin
the world would recognize, something that would make a difference?

I think this feeling is familiar to you, to me, to the greeter at Walmart, an
to the cashier at McDonald's. I believe that we all desire greatness and fulfillmen
in our cores of being, even if we don't know what that means for us yet.

It's a trope, but we all have our versions of success. I didn't know what min
was at the time, but I did know was that despite the positive momentum in m
life, I couldn't settle for less than I was capable of achieving. I had heard tons c
stories about kids my age and younger earning themselves hundreds of thousand
of dollars from their businesses, and they had all of the freedom in the world t
mold their lives to their liking—I wanted in.

So, I did it. I must have walked a mile in that little house before I pulled th
trigger, but I did it—I bought the course.

Betting big on yourself is a strange feeling. It's somehow easier to bet on
football game, a horse, or even a poker hand. When you bet on yourself, it's dc
or-die. Everything is in your control, and success or failure comes entirely by you
own doing. There is an immense feeling of freedom mixed with a dose of "wha
have I done?" but whether you find yourself confident or afraid, there is only on
course of action—to move forward.

I dove into the course, waking up early and staying up late to take note
and learn the material. The first item of action was to create a vision and a plan fc
execution. The following weekend, I skipped the big fraternity party and locke
myself in the library for two and a half days to avoid distraction. I must hav
seemed like such a loser, but that was the weekend my world changed.

That weekend, I hardly checked my phone. I visualized my dream life an
put it into a PDF that I printed and kept by my bedside. Once my dream life ha

een mapped out, I created a one-year plan to keep me on the right path, with etailed instructions on what to do each day for the next 365 days. In theory, all had to do was follow my own instructions to get what I wanted.

My plans changed about two weeks later when my boss sent me to a business narketing meetup to hear an expert speak on new marketing strategies. After ome tertiary research, I discovered that the speaker had spent one BILLION ollars in online ads. He was also running ads for the Golden State Warriors in neir prime, and he had worked with dozens of other Fortune 500 companies. prepped some questions, sat in the front, and took notes. That presentation hattered my paradigm of how the Internet worked.

After the presentation, I stuck around to say thank you and introduce nyself. I shook the lecturer's hand with all of the eager energy I could muster and itched my vision to him. It must have made an impression on him because he old me to apply for an internship, and I got the position.

I still remember the morning I went to work to tell my boss that I had to it the road, effectively forfeiting my guaranteed job after college. It was tough, ut I had to trust my gut and seize the opportunity.

Things accelerated from there. Within two weeks of meeting my mentor, was flying around the country, engaging with some of the biggest names in narketing on the planet, and working on international brands.

I flew out to California for a marketing conference where I met the organizer. Ie assigned me the position of lead marketing specialist for a professional sports eam and hired an international team under me. We were even featured as experts n training videos at GoDaddy's offices in Scottsdale. My mentor personally oached me, day in and day out, and I was learning faster than I ever had before.

The coming months tested me in every possible way. One night, while visiting mily back home, my brother and I were walking the dogs around 10:00 p.m. hen my phone rang. It was my mentor on the line. His plane had turned around n the way to a conference, and he needed me to fill in for him the next morning n New York City. I had never presented the material before, and my mentor was a 5-year industry veteran. How could I possibly fill his shoes? Nevertheless, I rushed ome, booked my flight, practiced until 4:00 a.m., and woke up to catch my plane at 5:00 a.m. I made it to the conference to deliver the presentation with about a hour to spare.

One time, I worked two back-to-back, 95-hour weeks in front of th computer, not counting bathroom breaks. Moments like these pushed me to ris to the occasion. I had to learn on the fly with limited time and focus and roll wit the punches. I also learned the power of a good mentor. For the first time, I sa the life lessons I had learned. These experiences must have shaved a good decad off my traditional learning curve—in business years, I would be pushing 40 soor

I took a semester off school to focus on work, but in conspiring fashio things came to a halt. I worked excessively, and my relationship floundered becaus of it. My mentor had taught me so much, but I couldn't keep up, and I steppe away. I did too little too late to save my relationship, my lease at the college hous was up, and I moved home without a job, no girlfriend, and a semester behind i school. To save money, I also stepped back from my fraternity, which would co me the friendships I'd spent so much time building. What had I *done*?

I tried to start a new business with some guys I had met on the road. T avoid the shame of returning to school as a failure, I took a semester of onlin classes from home at the same time. It wasn't long before the business ended i arguments, and I was forced to return to campus or lose another semester. Thos were dark months, and my new college house seemed to reflect the state of m spirit. I moved in with roommates who left food rotting on the ground next to th trash can. Talk about high-class living! I stayed up late, distracted by TV show and I even picked up smoking to affirm my internal dismay.

It was in those months that my bank account went all the way down to $ (actually less than that because I overdrew my debit card), and I had to ask m parents to cover my basic living expenses for a month. That hurt. It wasn't lon before that I was networking and meeting some of the most successful people i my industry. How had I sunk so low?

There were moments when I wanted to throw in the towel, finish m degree, and "get back on track." I even wrote a modified vision document th stated I would "finish my degree no matter what." I stopped trusting myself.

I couldn't bring myself to get a job, however. I couldn't "unsee" the success once had. I couldn't silence the burning question in my mind: "Why not me?"

urns out that a yearning spirit is not easily crushed. Instead of giving up, I picked myself up, started to network, and managed to secure some projects that helped pay my bills.

Then, I got a surprising message from my mentor, offering me a second chance. How could I say no?

I finished my semester at school and went back to work with my mentor. It was just as challenging as before, but I was prepared. We flew around the world and back, working on massive projects. On one trip, I expected to be in Vegas for a two-day conference but ended up staying away from home for two months. Now, *that* is rolling with the punches. I went coast-to-coast across the United States, overseas to Taiwan, and even as far as the Philippines. There were times I slept on airport floors between 18-hour, non-stop workdays, but it was fun. My mentor helped me to save several more years on my learning curve.

The time eventually came for me to leave the roost and go out on my own with my newly found confidence and stronger skillset.

It wasn't a direct path to true entrepreneurship, however. I worked temporarily with another marketing agency to get back on my feet, though my first few personal clients were so challenging that I almost threw in the towel again.

I thought that maybe if I got a job for some security, I could grow my business part-time until it was "safe" to go out on my own, so I applied for a job and got an interview right away. An hour later, I had talked my way through three levels of management to the director of marketing at a $275 million company. They offered me the job with an annual salary of $50,000 per year with benefits, paid vacation, flexible hours, and a "great opportunity" to earn a whopping 5% yearly raise. Now, I'm no mathematician, but 5% of $50,000 is only a couple hundred bucks extra per month *before* tax. That was when I knew that I could never work for anyone else. I knew that, if I focused my efforts, I could earn a 5% raise every day working for myself.

That was the last straw. I'd officially given up everything I once had—my degree, my girlfriend, my fraternity, my college friends, and my career—but something interesting happens when you abandon one path for another. At each major juncture along the way, you learn something new about yourself. Each of these lessons helped me mold and clarify what I want out of life, and I got close to my vision with each step.

I met another girl who is beautiful, intelligent, and kind. I realized that no one cared if I had a degree. I learned not to work for money, but to make money work for me. I have a better appreciation for the friends I've kept. I'm in fortunate position in that I have the ability to select the projects on which I want to work and the people with whom I want to work.

It's easy to follow the crowd. It's easy to do "what you're supposed to." It easy to dream about having a better life. It's hard to bet on yourself. It's hard to stick it out and do the work. It's hard to pick yourself back up and break free of the chains of fear and doubt.

I knew I would never realize my dreams if I followed a traditional path. It was only by going against the grain have I given myself the opportunities to turn my dreams into reality.

BIOGRAPHY

Ben Dahl is an author, speaker, and business coach who has helped Fortune 500 companies grow online. Having spent millions of dollars in marketing and leading international teams, Ben has the technical and leadership experience to produce massive results. With his expertise in marketing and operations he helps businesses expand through building scalable systems, uniting teams, and generating demand. Ben has spoken on international stages, led full-day workshops, and worked alongside industry leaders around the world to educate entrepreneurs on cutting-edge strategies for business growth. Ben believes that by helping others win, he can elevate more people to live life on their own terms. When Ben is not working, he enjoys long walks in nature, reading, and a good board game.

Contact Information
Facebook: https://www.facebook.com/BenDahlMarketing/

CHAPTER 6

THE ONE SECRET TO LONG LASTING FITNESS

By Bernard Yeo

S tand at a busy intersection and observe the people passing by. What do you notice? A significant number of people are overweight. In today's world, the internet and social media provide information about health and fitness in an instant, yet the number of overweight people is increasing.

If you struggle with being overweight or lack motivation for exercise, I might be able to help.

Being in a comfort zone makes us feel safe and certain in routine activities and habits, so we may feel that stepping out of this zone could bring unexpected risk and stress. For instance, if you've never been the exercising kind, you'll need the motivation to get started and stay on course, right?

Most of us know someone who had the sudden motivation to lose weight, whether it was to impress a girl or get in shape for the summer or a planned holiday. But once the girl moves on to be with someone else or when the event is over, the motivation disappears, and the weight gain returns.

You see, these motivations are external influences. It's not necessarily a bad thing. It is effective for jumpstarting a fitness program. I used to think all it required was enough motivation to act and succeed in getting healthy and fit. I

soon learned it also takes determination and willpower to stay motivated, whic
is why so many people give up after a while.

So, how do some people make keeping the weight off look so easy? How d
they stay so motivated for so long? What is the differentiating factor?

There is another element more powerful than motivation. And it is nc
another kind of motivation. I often wondered why I could stay motivated lon
enough to be successful at certain things while some of my friends couldn't. Ther
I came across research by Dr. Maxwell Maltz, a cosmetic surgeon. He noticed tha
after correcting imperfections on his patients' appearances, some still felt they wen
ugly, and this led to his discovery of self-image. In his book, Psycho-Cybernetic
he said, "A human being always acts and feels and performs in accordance wit
what he imagines to be true about himself and his environment." So, it wasn
what his patients saw when they looked in the mirror. It didn't matter becaus
they considered themselves ugly.

Self-image determines the actions and decisions a person makes every da
For example, someone might have a goal to lose weight, but he continuousl
sabotages his efforts by overeating sugary foods. Why is that? His self-image
that of an overweight person and so his subconscious mind will consistently ac
in accordance with his self-image.

Effective weight management starts with motivation, but it won't sustai
you. You need to program your subconscious mind and develop a good self-imag
to be successful in the long term.

Looking back on my life as an example, I started smoking in my early thirtie
It probably started with friends over at my house. They wanted to smoke, and
wanted to be social. Soon I was taking smoke breaks with my work colleagu
as well. But, after a few months, I didn't feel good about smoking. I felt that
wasn't me. Unbeknown to me at the time, it was probably Dr. Maltz's influenc
from the power of self-image. Perhaps my self-image of being a non-smoker cam
from my father. He smoked ever since I knew him and then he passed away fror
cancer when he was only fifty-one years old. Prior to discovering he had cancer, h
engineering company still had hundreds of thousands of dollars owing to the bank
for machinery leasing, loans, and recurring costs in operating a factory. My mothe
my brothers, and I had to pick up from where he left off as it was our only sourc

f income. It was terrifying because we didn't know anything about operating a business. Losing him was the hardest episode of my life and it was a shame that he couldn't teach us any business skills in time.

Not to brag, but I found it wasn't difficult for me to quit smoking as I had no withdrawal symptoms or nicotine cravings. So, despite the many people around me who smoke, I couldn't be influenced for long. While people normally fail to quit smoking, you can say that I *failed* in smoking!

Another significant event in my life was when I wanted to lose weight in December 2010. I was already in my late thirties and I had not exercised for years. While I was deciding on what to do, I found out that my cousin, Thomas, had just finished a full marathon. Ever since I was a teenager, I admired people who ran a full 42.196 km. I couldn't even run 5 km without stopping a few times. So, my cousin's success inspired me to get into running.

My idea of succeeding was to totally immerse myself in running. First, I set a goal to run a marathon in six months. Then, I bought a book on the beginner's guide to running a marathon. I started to train according to the plan in the book with almost no deviation. I watched proper running techniques on YouTube, signed up for shorter races leading up to the big event, and I became aware of my food choices. I imagined myself running like Ancient Greek messengers delivering letters in times of war.

On marathon day, it was a tough and hot race. I had cramps in muscles I never knew existed. But I completed the race in five hours and one minute.

Over the next few years, I would run more marathons and even a 100 km ultramarathon. In 2018, I decided to shift from running to lifting weights.

In my marathon example, I was initially motivated to run a marathon in six months. I was motivated by my cousin's success. But, I also totally immersed myself in the sport, so much so that being a long-distance runner formed part of my self-image, which made me get out there to train, regardless if it was too hot or raining.

Now, we circle back to my original promise to you - to help you be successful in your fitness journey. I recommend you get started by motivating yourself and developing the self-image for long-lasting change. How long should you keep yourself motivated – until you achieved your goal and transformed you self-image.

Start your fitness journey with a reason. For me, it was my wife an children. I never want them to experience what I went through with my father death. Write a letter to yourself (don't type on a computer) and tell yourself wh you want to be fit. The letter can be any length, but the longer it is, the bette I want you to make a *promise* to yourself that you will achieve your goal. I sa promise because breaking promises is more emotional than just missing a goal. have taken out letters to myself written months ago and whenever I read them, get emotionally charged.

Another powerful technique is to announce your goals on social media lik Facebook. Letting all your friends know and holding yourself accountable can b incredibly powerful. You will get a lot of motivation and encouragement fror your friends. Similarly, with your letter, on Facebook, you are promising you friends.

Build your self-image. Dr. Maltz said to change our self-image, we must us our imagination. By imagining a new healthier version of ourselves, our actior will be redirected to make it come true.

It can be hard to imagine because we are preoccupied with distractin thoughts, so meditation can be effective through implementing more of ou senses to achieve our goals. So, here's what I want you to do: Take your self-imag vision from the back of your mind and put it in front of your eyes by writing out on paper. Again, there's something real about the act of writing things dowr You employ the sense of sight, touch and hearing your written words in you mind. Create a vision of what you want to be. Put it on your desk or refrigerato and look at it everyday.

When You Don't Feel Motivated

Here's the other side to achieving your goals. There will be days where you don feel motivated to do anything. You won't feel like going to the gym or for a rur I've faced laziness and procrastination too. There are some people who sugge dressing in a gym or running attire is motivating to get going. If you find a effective technique, then use it.

Here's what worked for me. When I was a runner, I told myself I'll only run for five minutes. If after 5 minutes I don't feel like running anymore, I'll stop. But, after five minutes if I feel like I want to continue, then I will run for another five minutes. Then I evaluate again if I want to continue or stop. I have run extra distances because of this mind hack. And, if your exercise is at the gym, tell yourself to go but only commit to do the warmup sets of your favorite muscle group, then decide if you want to continue the workout or not. You haven't failed if you stop after five minutes. Think of it as a sloppy day and let it go.

Another way to beat motivation (or lack thereof) is to integrate fitness into your life. Consider using resistance bands while watching television, set exercise time using calendar appointments, or have friends pick you up at scheduled times to go to the gym. Stick to these ideas and I promise you, you'll see the change in your self-image.

I want to close this chapter with the story about the scorpion and the frog. You may have heard of it, but I have a different view. The insert below is from Wikipedia:

A scorpion asks a frog to carry it across a river. The frog hesitates, afraid of being stung by the scorpion, but the scorpion argues that if it did that, they would both drown. The frog considers this argument sensible and agrees to transport the scorpion. The scorpion climbs onto the frog's back and the frog begins to swim, but midway across the river, the scorpion stings the frog, dooming them both. The dying frog asks the scorpion why it stung, to which the scorpion replies, "I couldn't help it. It's in my nature."

Just like it is the scorpion's nature to sting, you must establish a healthy self-image with fitness in your nature. If you do, you will never have to struggle with weight issues again.

BIOGRAPHY

Bernard Yeo is known for his love for personal development and dedication to personal fitness. Having run marathons for several years and switching to weight training, he has redirected his passion for coaching others on how to fight the battle of the bulge and gain fitness. With years of virtual traveling overseas and YouTube on his belt, he now makes actual adventurous and challenging trips with his ex-classmates every year. Bernard lives with his wife and two sons in Kuala Lumpur, Malaysia.

Contact Information
Facebook: https://www.facebook.com/BernardYeo
Instagram: https://www.instagram.com/justdoit.mindset/

CHAPTER 7

NEVER ENDING JOURNEY

By Carolyn V. Anderson

S uccess for me continues to be a never-ending journey of challenges followed by favorable outcomes. Pulling back the covers and getting out of my warm bed turned out to be the biggest challenge on this cold winter morning. I once worked for a successful attorney who told me that success started with waking up and getting out of bed every day with an attitude of gratitude. Years later, when I was going through the divorce process, remembering his words and enforcing that positive attitude saved me from falling into depression.

According to the dictionary sitting beside my computer, the word "success" has more than one meaning. Apart from gaining wealth and fame, it also describes success as achieving a favorable or desired result. The point is if you are happy with your outcome, you are successful.

For as long as I can remember, I liked sharing anything beautiful or unusual that I saw in the world around me. My father, an artist, taught me to sketch and reproduce my interpretation of the surroundings on paper.

I was immersed in sketching, doing it as often as I could find the time, thereby improving my skills. But the thought of making money from my art never occurred to me. In high school, an advertising agency collaborated with our school's art department and sponsored a poster contest with cash prizes.

The agency was in search of ideas for billboard advertisements for its clients. The design had to be simple but large enough for drivers and passengers in vehicles on the highway to see and read the message in a flash.

Our art teachers provided the poster boards and poster paint. I visualized my design and then sat down with paint colors to sketch and paint. When our posters were completed, the teachers submitted them to the agency's team for decision.

On the day of the contest results, we all gathered in the school's auditorium. The first poster displayed on the stage was the poster for third prize. I recognized my poster and heard my name being called. I walked up to the stage with bounce in my steps and a smile on my face to receive my envelope of cash.

As the second and the first prize winners received their envelopes, a sense of curiosity directed my attention to the other winning posters. I realized that even though I had submitted a well-thought-out and artistically-done poster, the subject of the other two winners was better aligned with the vision of the agency's clients.

First lesson learned—*always give the client what they are looking for.*

DEVELOPING SKILLS

I pursued my passion in college and majored in art and design. I also picked up new skills in architecture, blueprint layouts, and exterior and interior designs. In my oil painting class, our Instructor challenged us to use color to show line and movement on a new canvas. I had been up the previous night studying for an exam in my next class, so I chose to paint a subject similar to what I had studied. created something different from my usual work. By doing so, I gave him exactly what he was looking for, and not surprisingly, that painting ended up in the university's gallery.

In one of my design classes, the Instructor gave us the taste of creating "light and dark" designs on photo paper. I was enchanted with the developing process in the darkroom. Seeing the images come to life in the developing tray

eignited my passion for recreating beauty around me. It was a much quicker way
o share images that would make others smile.

After college, as we stepped into the real world, only office desk jobs were
vailable to women at that time. I was good at answering phones and could type,
o a job downtown was not hard to find. I started looking for photography classes
lose to work as I did not want to put my new passion on hold.

I learned to be aware of the lighting and contrasting color shades while
aking black and white photos. Acquiring new tricks of developing photographs,
 experimented with my grandfather's 35-millimeter camera with a retractable
billow." I took photos during my lunch hours and sometimes after work.

Grateful that I had a salary and paychecks to rely on

uch was my passion that I started saving money to purchase equipment for
eveloping photos. It wasn't long afterward that my closest friend and I made
lans to fly to the New York World's Fair later that year. I was still living at home
vhen my parents decided to move closer to my grandmother. As I wanted to
nove with them, I purchased an automobile to commute to work. In an effort
o save money, my girlfriend and I drove to New York from Michigan in my new
Chevy. With a newly-purchased Kodak Instamatic camera, which automatically
dvanced each frame after the shutter closed, our journey began.

I had enjoyed traveling to several states and Canada before college, so this
vas a much-anticipated trip. We drove straight to our hotel in New York. Parking
ny car in the hotel's garage, we relied on the subway system to get us to the
air and back. Everywhere we went, my camera accompanied me. I gained an
ppreciation for the quick shutter movement when we took the "ski lift" above
he fairgrounds from one end to the other. I had a lot of photos developed by
omeone else and put together a photo album to show to family and friends who
therwise would never see the World's Fair.

Another detour before building a darkroom

 had finally saved enough money to purchase the necessary equipment for my
arkroom. But by the time the equipment arrived, I had fallen in love and was

planning my wedding. So, it went to storage at my parent's house.

I hadn't been to San Francisco since I was seventeen. My husband's frien lived there, so we flew to San Francisco for our honeymoon. I carried one c my cameras along on our tours in and outside the city and visited sights that missed on my first time there. On the weekend, we flew down to Los Angeles t visit my sister-in-law's husband. She had come to our wedding, but her husban could not get off work to travel. It was the perfect opportunity to capture the cit in its full spirit. The next week, we drove to San Diego—I had never been ther and was eager to take photos by the water. A few days later, we were homewar bound flying out of the Los Angeles airport. Yet again, I sent the film out to b developed, but at the back of my mind, I was dreaming of my darkroom.

We rented an inexpensive apartment, which allowed us to save for a depos on a home we eventually purchased. Our firstborn was five months old when w moved into our new home. There, I set up a darkroom and went to work in it, bu it proved difficult. When our second child was born, it became almost impossib to make use of the darkroom. Remembering something I heard long ago, "Ou of something negative comes something positive." I realized I still had my camer and knew where I could have my film developed. I was grateful to watch m children grow up and capture those precious moments on film.

When my children were in school, I opened up my darkroom. Th photographs I developed were mostly shared as gifts; that would put a smile o the recipient's faces. The success I achieved could not be evaluated monetarily.

Several years later, in the process of divorce, I could no longer afford th cost involved in photography. I had a son and daughter in their mid-teens an a job that barely paid the bills. The photos and processing were not paying fo themselves, so I had to shut it all down.

The thought of starting afresh and reopening my darkroom began to tak shape when my children ventured out on their own. But without a plan, m enthusiasm for the process wavered. Out of the blue, one of my girlfriends aske me to share a booth with her at a local street fair. I created greeting cards to matc her crafted door hangers—this plan ended up being mutually beneficial. So, w made plans to do it again the following year, and my daughter encouraged me t sell my photos this time.

As there were several craft booths selling photos, I decided to place my lack and white photos on greeting cards. A friend of mine owned a printing shop with her husband, so I asked her for help. She showed me how to do the layouts, which they ran through the press on heavy stock paper. Then they scored the seam to be folded, and it was ready for the next step. I purchased envelopes for the cards and applied for a copyright. Grateful for her help, I suggested she keep a few cards to display as samples for their customers.

At the last moment, my booth partner backed out. With the help of friends and the women in the two booths around me, I set up my display. Pricing the "photocards" as single cards, I also sold them in packages of ten. I helped the two women next to me by watching their booths whenever they needed a break. They did the same for me. By the end of the two-day fair, the three of us had become friends. For the next four years, we requested the same spaces next to each other.

Battling the rainy clouds, the sun shone brightly on the day of the craft show. I was pleased with the successful sales of the cards. Michigan Lighthouse photoprints drew the most attention—coincidentally, they were my favorite. Now a new journey was materializing; to find other lighthouse enthusiasts and join them in visiting and photographing lighthouses.

I realized that success achieved through working with others is undoubtedly more fun. Finally, I had found an opportunity that made a positive difference in the lives of others. I discovered that as a team, we reached more people, identified their needs, and helped them find solutions. It was a whole new level of success beyond our expectations. When you only focus on personal success, you limit yourself. When each member of the team develops another person, and that person develops another who, in turn, develops the next, and the next, you will have a chain of people, a team, working toward a common goal.

I have often read that "You are the average of the five people you spend the most time with." Often visiting The Henry Ford Museum, old photos of three successful men come to mind—Thomas Edison, Henry Ford, and Harvey Firestone, who all shared a strong friendship. Surround yourself with the right people and build a network of successful people as your support group. The results may surprise you.

BIOGRAPHY

At a time in Carolyn's life, when most people retire, she is infused with a strong impulse to see what is around the next corner. She hopes that her story inspires you to pursue your dreams with passion despite the challenges life throws at you. She believes that "You only fail if you quit." She acquired her writing skills with the help of her high school journalism teacher. Carolyn recently joined other best-selling authors in *The Art and Science of Success, Volume 5,* with her chapter "Finding Success Every Day." She learned teamwork and leadership skills through local and national organizations: parent-teachers association, 6-Area Coalition for Community Mental Health Board of Directors, and Parents Without Partners (as a program and education leader).

Contact Information
Facebook: https://www.facebook.com/CarolynsVerve

CHAPTER 8

FACE YOUR GRIZZLY BEAR

By Chris McIntosh

You are squatting on the bank of a snowy stream, filling your water bottle. As you watch the water flow into your bottle, a thought engulfs your mind—you will be forever lost in this unforsaken wilderness and die. You will never be rescued. Then, images of your family back home come flooding in. Your children need you to teach them about life. They are counting on you. And they have no idea where you are at this moment. Something kicks in, and you begin to strategize your way out of your situation, blaming yourself for getting into it in the first place. You hope to get rescued, for everything you have tried so far that didn't work. As your belly reminds you that it has been too long since your last meal, you rack your brain to find food and survive another night without freezing to death. You look down and see your tired reflection in the stream and think, "If I follow this, maybe it will show me a way out."

As your water bottle is almost full, you hear a noise in the bushes, upstream from where you are squatting. You turn, look up, and your eyes lock with a grizzly bear, who is now casually strolling toward you. The bear you thought you had escaped from days earlier, has found you again. Now, he is approaching you directly, and he is not coming to be your friend. Fear suddenly consumes you and dropping your bottle, *you run*!

We are all created with a purpose, destined to do great things in our live: But why is it that most people lead what Henry David Thoreau called Lives c Quiet Desperation? For most people, the biggest regret at the end of their days not the things they did and failed at, but those they were too afraid of doing. Nc speaking up for themselves, not doing *that* thing they always wanted to do, no approaching the person who made their hearts flutter, or not making amends wit a family member constitute some of those regrets. People regret being risk-avers and not starting that business they had always dreamed of; not taking enoug vacations; not living the lives they were destined and created to live; of not havin the courage to live lives they wanted instead of the lives others expected them t live; and of working hard all of their lives only to build someone else's busines and someone else's dream.

Yet again, you have gotten away from the grizzly bear. But this time, yo realize that it is only temporary—he will find you again. As long as you are i his world, he will sniff you out. You are no longer thinking about being rescuec about getting to a place of freedom. All you can think about is how this grizzl bear is going to take you out, and when it will happen.

As you're contemplating your demise, your thoughts revert to your futur to your family, to the things you still need to accomplish in this world, and a that moment, you make a decision—I must face this grizzly bear; I must kill th grizzly bear. How can you ever do that when all you have is a small pocket knif Surely, a pocket knife could never penetrate deep enough into the bear's hide t do any lethal damage, but then you remember reading about how others had slai grizzly bears with nothing more than a spear.

We all have so much potential to achieve great things in our lives, bu we've built these invisible and internal barriers. We are a powerhouse of so muc information, skills learned through the books we have read, and from the life w have been living. Courses bought, money invested in the boot camps—yet we sti do not have the success we deserve.

Why is it that success evades you? Is it because you didn't buy the righ course, or you don't have the right information? Perhaps you didn't read the righ book, or you just weren't born into the right family. The answer to all of thes questions is "no." You have not yet arrived because there are grizzly bears in you fe. Each time you begin to tread on the path of success, the grizzly bear is right here, waiting for you and ready to devour you. Ultimately, fear grips you, and *ou run!*

One of the most popular acronyms for fear is "False Evidence Appearing .eal." I have heard another one—"Forget Everything and Run." Fear is a powerful motion and a primal instinct, which compels one to *run* in the face of danger. consumes you, and if you let it control you, it ends up controlling your life. ventually, you begin to justify the fear and consider it a new norm. "Living by efault"—our whole lives, we are programmed to live a certain way. The problem 'ith a default way of life is that it is just too easy. It is too easy to show up every ay at the job you hate. But we justify it by saying, "At least, it's a paycheck." We re programmed to go to school and get good grades so that we can go to college nd receive a degree (along with a mountain of student debt). And why do we eed a degree? To get a job, of course, and they pay you just enough so you won't uit, and of course, you work just hard enough so you won't get fired. Besides, they have great benefits," you say. I call this "the golden handcuffs."

Now, there's nothing wrong with getting a degree and having a job. But not aving a plan to get out of that job when you want, is wrong. The greatest country the world, the United States of America, is the most prosperous country in the orld. People risk everything, including their own lives, to get there. Then why is that even at the age of sixty-five, nine out of ten Americans will be living at or elow the poverty line? Because living by default is easy. Even right now, as I write his, the economy is booming, yet many Americans will come up short when it omes to retirement income. The idea of being a greeter at a Walmart, when you hould be enjoying your golden years, is not exactly enticing. According to the ension Rights Center, half of all Americans at the age of sixty-five or older have ncomes of less than $24,224 a year—far less than the amount most need to meet heir day-to-day living and health care expenses. Yet, I am grateful for companies ke Walmart that are willing to employ the elderly in our society who fall in the rap of a "default life."

"Face Everything And Rise"—my favorite acronym for fear. We all have rizzly bears or fear in our lives, but how we deal with that fear determines our uture. The only way to design your life instead of living by default is to first slay

the grizzly bear in your life. I am no different: I bought the books, the course
invested in boot camps, but I never had any success. That is until I realized that m
success had nothing to do with the information I had purchased. Merely hoardin
information or knowledge wasn't enough; I had to take action. Most people
inability to take action reflects their deepest fears, current behaviors, curren
beliefs, and operating norms. Their assumptions and rigid patterns prevent ther
from living by design, and they resist any change in their lives. I once heard tha
the only person who likes change is a baby with a wet diaper. I was at a place in m
life when I realized that I had grizzly bears preventing me from making chang
and harvesting my true potential.

I had humble beginnings, so I needed to overcome the invisible barriers t
achieve success. As a young child, I often saw my mother rip pieces of paper calle
food stamps out of a book, as we didn't have enough money to buy groceries. Th
embarrassment of standing in line in that grocery store is still fresh in my mind
My father refused to go with my mother as he could not bear the humiliation.
don't have a college degree—my parents could hardly afford food, much less pa
for college. I'm the oldest of six kids. My dad was in the timber industry—he wa
a logger, or as some people call it, a lumberjack. I love my mom and dad, an
they did the very best they could with what they had. Unbeknownst to them, the
lived a life of default. Our broken educational system fixates on how to score
job. To my parents, they did everything right—my dad was and still is a very har
worker. After the Vietnam War, my dad did the honorable thing that every fathe
does. He went to get a job to provide for his growing family. He didn't have
college degree either, so he did exactly what his dad had done, and that was to g
to work in the timber industry. And he taught me how to do the same—to
hard worker—and that's what I did. I worked hard, and I thought that the harde
I worked, the more ahead I would get. So, I followed after my father. My dad di
give me some advice, though. He said, "Son, don't go into the Army and lear
how to be a mercenary. Instead, go into the Air Force so you will at least learn
skill. So, you won't have to work in the woods your whole life."

Following his advice, I went into the Air Force. Please, don't get m
wrong—I am grateful for all branches of the military. It is because of our militar
that our country is as great as it is, and we have the freedom to choose to live b

esign. I would recommend my boys to serve in the military, as you can learn so
much about yourself and discipline from the armed forces, but I also teach my
children to live by design.

We all have defining moments in our lives. Reading this book could be
your defining moment. I encountered mine during a conversation with a letter
carrier. After getting out of the Air Force, I held various jobs, including working
in the woods as a lumberjack. While working as a letter carrier at the post office,
I met another letter carrier who had been working at that post office longer than
I had been alive. At that point in time, I thought I had finally arrived. I had a
government job—there was no way I could get fired, and the pay was really good.
When I found out that this letter carrier had been delivering mail longer than I
had been alive, I was blown away. I was in my early thirties, and the conversation
had come to the place where I asked him how much money he made annually.

That question and his response was my defining moment. When he told
me how much he earned, I realized that I could no longer work for the post office.
At that time, I was earning more money than him on an annual basis. How could
I be making more money, having only been at the post office for a short four years
than someone who had been there for thirty-plus years? I blindly followed what
my dad had taught me, and I worked hard.

> "If you don't find a way to make money while
> you sleep, you will work until you die."
> —Warren Buffett

I was trading time for money. I worked so hard that I requested to be on what was
called the ODL, the Overtime Desired List. This concept may sound foreign to
some: I worked ten to twelve hours a day, six days a week, and thus, I made more
money on an annual basis than a thirty-year US postal worker who only worked
a forty-hour week. But as is customary, my standard of living had adjusted to
the money I was making, and I was not getting ahead financially. It hit me that
I was not willing to work ten to twelve hours a day, six days a week for the rest
of my life. I had a young daughter at home, Makayla, I adored her, and I wanted
more children. I remember that I didn't have a lot of time with my dad because
he worked so much, but I treasured what little time I had with him, which was

usually only on the weekends. I cherish the time that we spent hunting, camping, and fishing together. I fondly recall that on weekends he would take me with him to the gym, and we would play a game of pickup basketball with all of his friends. I wanted to spend more time with my family and wanted that for my children, so I quit the post office to pursue a business that I hoped would get me to the land of financial freedom. Soon after, the grizzly bear came. Things got bad. I got divorced. Life turned upside down.

In the movie, *The Edge*, which I highly recommend you watch, Anthony Hopkins is being chased by a grizzly bear. He realizes that his only option is to kill the grizzly bear. It is the statement that he makes in the movie that changed my life, as I hope for this book to change yours.

He says, "What one man can do, so can another." I had long realized that I was destined for success in my life; so, all I needed to do was to learn what others have done to find success and then replicate it. I wanted to leave a legacy for generations to come, so investing in real estate made sense. For me, real estate investing was the vehicle through which I would create a passive income and free up my time. Over time, I learned what others had done to gain success, not just in real estate—because if it was easy, everyone would be doing it—but in life.

We all have grizzly bears that chase us down and prevent us from taking action, from getting to that place of ultimate success, and it is very scary. Your choice, whether you *Forget Everything And Run*, or *Face Everything And Rise*, makes all the difference. Remember, you do not have to carry the burden all by yourself. "What one man can do, so can another." Face your fears, slay your grizzly bear, and change your life. Stop living by default and instead choose a life of design. If you won't do it for yourself, do it for your family, for your legacy. Is it scary? Yes. But you can do it. I believe in you.

BIOGRAPHY

Chris McIntosh has been an entrepreneur for over fifteen years. He has coached, mentored, and inspired hundreds of entrepreneurs and real estate investors over the last decade. He founded and is currently the president of the longest-running real estate investing club in his hometown of Spokane, Washington. He manages a multi-million-dollar real estate portfolio and helps others get into the game of business ownership and real estate investment. His mission is to inspire others and empower them with universal truths to lead a life of design. He is the proud father of Makayla, Austin, Noah, Caleb, and Jessica.

Contact Information
Facebook: https://www.facebook.com/mcintoc
Instagram: https://www.instagram.com/tip.real.estate/
Website: http://www.nextgenrei.com

CHAPTER 9

OVERCOMER

By Cindy Cavazos

I remember from a young age having to take care of my brother, who was a year younger than me, as well as a three-year-old child. At the time, it was just my brother, my mother and I; I didn't have a father in my life and knew nothing about him. The only other family I had was an aunt. My mom was single who often worked nights, so I was left alone to care for my brother and anyone else who was with us, and usually, instructions were left for me to warm or cook dinner. We must have been on food stamps because I remember the book of play money. We also moved around often, so I don't have any childhood friends.

One night, while my mom was at work, someone broke into our apartment. I was lifted from my bed and taken to another room. I woke up with a pillow over my face hearing whispers, while a cold metal object was pressed to my forehead. It was a gun. I couldn't see the man, but he was molesting me. When my mom came home, she found her gun had been taken with other valuables. I said I was okay after the incident, and it was never mentioned again. I was eight or nine years old at the time.

Later, when I had children, I did not leave them home alone until they were eighteen.

When I was nine, my mom met a Greek man, and they had a daughter, my sister, who I took care of since she was two weeks old. I remember staying up all night when she had colic. My mom was at work, and I had school the next morning. It was just our routine. My brother and I looked after our sister for many years while my mom worked. I recall sitting on the door frame of our 2-bedroom apartment in Houston with my siblings as the sun set because the light between our apartment door and neighbor's door was the only light we had. It wasn't a power outage. The light bill hadn't been paid. I think a neighbor called my mom to let her know our lights were out.

Throughout my life, my mom worked 2 to 3 jobs to make ends meet. She missed out on holidays, our birthdays, including her own, as well as Mother Day. She also missed our school functions. During a school production of Hansel and Gretel where I played Gretel, I remember standing on the stage looking for my mom and nearly forgot my lines while looking for her in the ocean of faces. She wasn't there.

My brother and I were due to go on a field trip, and although I don't remember if it was through the church or school, I do remember asking my mom repeatedly to wake up and drive us there. We were late, and they were going to leave without us, but she couldn't wake up. When I came back into her room, she was trying to place her legs through a paper bag, thinking they were pants because she was still asleep. We eventually managed to wake her, and we made it to our field trip, but I will never get that image of my sleep-deprived mom out of my mind.

It was sometime in junior high when my mother met my second stepfather who was all smiles at first. He worked and helped my mom with bills, and he too had a daughter, my youngest sister. He showed my siblings love, but he was addicted to drugs and alcohol. To this day, I don't know the substance he was taking. I just remember the syringes and glass pipes.

The abuse was subtle at first, which then started escalating from corporal punishment to verbal abuse to outright hitting me. It was during high school either as a freshman or sophomore, when my relationship with God blossomed thanks to two young school friends. They invited me to a church where I started building a relationship with God who I adopted as my father since I didn't have one. On one occasion, my friends came to pick me up for church and my

epfather said, "The bitches are here for you." My stomach turned. How could he
all the people who shed love and light into my life such foul names?

He had been drinking straight for days and had lost his job. One night he
ame into my room and hit me for no reason while sitting next to my sister. I
alled my mom and he denied hitting me. A screaming match followed and he
nreatened to kill us. He then left the house, and I told my mother I wasn't waiting
or him to return to kill us, so I was leaving. She packed our clothes and we all left
or a friend's house, where we stayed until my mom got a new apartment. After
nonths had passed, my mom told me that my stepfather was coming back to be
art of our family. I told her that if she chose him over us that I would leave when
turned eighteen; I was only sixteen at the time. She picked him.

We moved so much during my childhood that I couldn't tell you how many
chools we attended. I asked my mom to let me go to the same high school for
ll four years, but she broke that promise when she decided to move our family
o Florida for a business venture that summer. I left the few friends I had where
managed to be part of the drill team and played varsity soccer as a sophomore.
Now, all of that was over and I had to start new. I tried to stay behind with my
hurch family but my mom wouldn't allow it. I cried the whole drive to Florida.

Even though my stepfather had stopped drinking, he was still verbally
busive. I wasn't even allowed to have an open-air vent in my room; he would
ome into my room and close the vent. So one time, I removed the whole vent
om the wall, and he ransacked my room looking for it. I started working as a
ashier at the local grocery store and I needed to wash my work apron frequently
ecause it got soiled easily with milk, raw meat, fruits, and vegetables. Yet, I was
nly allowed to use our washer and dryer once a week. Another time, I didn't wash
ne dishes properly at home and my mom came to my work to look for me. I hid
om her and didn't go home that night. I stayed with aunt instead. Eventually I
eturned home.

I stayed busy, filling my time with school, work, and gym. There was a law
chool close by that I contemplated attending after graduating from high school.
asked my mom if I could, and she told me to ask my stepfather, the same man
vho bullied me daily. I knew then that I had no future in that household. I saved
noney to return to Houston and start my life there. I turned eighteen in the June

before my senior year and told my mom I already purchased a bus ticket back to Houston and that she could not stop me from leaving. My stepfather and my mom sat me down, and he confessed and apologized in front of my mother, saying he had purposely made my life miserable. I believe this was my mom's attempt to get me to stay, but I knew where her loyalties were, and they weren't with me. I left my siblings and my mother, but I was ready to live a life without abuse.

That summer, I lived with a church family back in Houston, and circumstances made it difficult for me to enroll in school and finish my senior year. It was not easy to have my school records transferred as I needed the paperwork I didn't have. One day my church family said they were moving and no longer had room for me. I found my stuff in a bag at the church when I returned from youth church retreat and found that my money had coincidentally run out too. I would contribute financially and do things like take the family out to eat and help pay for car repairs if they didn't have money, so I felt they used me until I was left penniless. I didn't have a car or a bike, so I had to depend on other people to give me rides. I asked a church friend if I could live with her; she was staying with her boyfriend's family. This arrangement didn't last long, so we both stayed with her mom who was living with another family. I didn't have any relatives in Houston just church family. I moved from home to home and finally decided to go live with my grandmother in Monterrey, Mexico to try finish my senior year there. I applied to the local school, but they needed my school paperwork. I begged my mom to send it, and although she said she did, the papers never made it to the school. I worked as a teacher and a telephone operator to offset expenses and took a bus everywhere I needed to go.

Meanwhile, my mother moved back to Houston. I wanted to finish my school so badly that I moved back to my mom in Houston, despite the fact that facing my stepfather would make me ill. With my stepfather's presence, I continued to be an awful living situation. I got a job in the same mall as my mom so we could share rides to and from work, but my stepfather said that I had to find my own ride. He would leave me there on the sidewalk, stranded at 10 pm as he drove away with my mom. There was no public transport system anywhere near there, and I was forced to ask strangers for rides or call taxis. Day-to-day life was challenging.

My stepfather wanted me to start paying rent. One evening, there was an argument, I don't even remember what it was about, but I just packed a small bag and started walking. I had a high school friend pick me up and I lived with him. We became romantically involved but it ended after a phone call between him and another girl where he denied my existence, while I was living there. We fought and he threw me out. I didn't have anywhere to go; I was only eighteen.

I looked in the Yellow Pages and found the Covenant House in Houston where he dropped me off.

The shelter wanted me to take a GED course, but I refused and went to the local high school where the school counselor wrote a letter to the shelter stating they would allow me to finish my school year. The shelter let me continue living there while I went to school, but it wasn't easy. I had to share a room with three strangers. I had hundreds of dollars, clothing, and sentimental jewelry stolen from me. I walked into my room once to find a guy shooting up drugs. I worked, went to school, and lived in the shelter, which had very strict rules. Some of the residents could not adhere to the rules and were either kicked out or left of their own accord. Some of them, male and female, were consumed by the streets of Houston and turned to prostitution. I cried every night that I was there.

Another church family reached out and explained they were willing to cosign an apartment for me. After living in the shelter for three months, I was able to leave and lease my first apartment with the cosigner's help. I started working as a waitress nearby and managed to pay all my bills on my own. I was still going to school to finish out the year and graduate, but to do so, I had to take two buses from southwest Houston to the inner-city high school, which took over an hour. Then, a family friend gave me a '78 Chevrolet Monte Carlo to drive to school and work. It was an old car that was expensive to maintain, but it was still better than waiting for a bus in the rain. To finish my high school education, I had to take a night school class at MacArthur High School on the northeast side of town where there were regular drive-bys and high gang activity. I fitted right in with my '78 Monte Carlo and felt like I was in East Los Angeles.

I graduated from high school with an honors diploma. I didn't attend graduation because I didn't know anyone in the school and knew nobody who would come support me. After the first six months of living alone, I was able to transfer the lease for my apartment into my name solely. The boyfriend I live with before the shelter, moved in with me and that was the beginning of a 20-year abusive and loveless relationship. I went from waitressing to working as a leasing agent in the office of the apartment complex where I lived. I took a year off from school to figure out what I wanted to study. The Monte Carlo engine died on me around the same time my stepfather did the same.

My mom called to tell me that my stepfather came home and was throwing up blood on the driveway. He was hospitalized and given a few days to live. My mom requested I go to see him, but I didn't want to; however, she urged me to go and I eventually relented. When I entered his room, he immediately sat up in bed, moving his arms and legs up and down uncoordinated. Obviously, he wanted to say something to me or even hit me one last time, but he couldn't utter one intelligible word. He died a few days later, and my siblings and mother were left alone once again.

I wanted to become an architect and decided to study electrical engineering at ITT. I worked nine to five and then attend school six to ten, Monday through to Friday. I was at the top of my class in college but in 1998, I became pregnant with twin daughters--one of the biggest blessings from God. I didn't think it was logical for me to pursue electrical engineering anymore because I was not going to put two babies in daycare. My daughters were born healthy. Their father and I decided I would continue to work because I made more money and had more benefits, and he would stay home with the twins. But, after about a month, I was ready to quit and be home with my daughters. We knew if we wanted to provide a future for our kids, we would either both have to work or move to Mexico where life was cheaper. Well, we saved, packed up and went to Mexico. I stayed home with the 2-year-old twins while their dad worked as a schoolteacher and gave private English lessons on the side. Yet, we still didn't have enough for food. rented out our PlayStation in 30-minute intervals, then added snacks and drinks but even then, the profit was just enough for us to eat. We sold our belongings at flea markets; we did what we could to put food on the table. God never let us go hungry. When we literally didn't have a dime to our name, a neighbor would come by and offer us a plate of food.

We had a very loyal customer who was ten years old, and I could always count on him to rent the PlayStation for 30 minutes every morning so that I could buy milk or eggs for the twins. It was interesting as this child was bullied because his mother would pick through everyone's trash to recycle paper, metal, plastic, and glass. He had nine siblings and his mother put the older children through college, and they were now lawyers and engineers. Even though he was bullied, he had more money in his pocket than any of the other kids, and they would often borrow from him as well as bully him. I favored this child. I treated him like my son and hated leaving him. My mom had put a bug in my ear about having another child soon, so I prayed that God would bless us with a son. I specifically asked for one boy, not two; otherwise I would have to sit on the floor of the car because we wouldn't have any more space for two extra car seats! Within three months, I was pregnant.

After the tragic event of 9/11, we returned home, and in the following month, our family was back in Houston. We were living with my husband's mother and brother, and that's when I began to realize where his loyalties lay. I tried to leave with my daughters, but his mother convinced me to stay. I shouldn't have. I should have walked away and never looked back. That's when I knew I had to make enough money to support myself and my children. I started the college enrollment process, but I didn't want to start until my son was a year old. My friends and family discouraged my return to school and discouraged me from becoming a nurse because of how hard it would be with three children.

I finished nursing school in May 2006 and graduated with honors. I worked hard as a nurse and encouraged the father of my children to go to school. He began his college education shortly afterward, but it took him six years to finish, during which time he did not work. After he graduated, he couldn't find a job. No one would hire him. I was so blinded, I made excuses, but ultimately, I didn't know any better. I didn't have a father other than God. I didn't have uncles or any good man in my life, just abusive stepfathers. I didn't see the red flags even though everyone who knew us did, and they tried to warn me. When he choked me for the first and last time, I moved out but I didn't file for divorce because I had done that before and lost a lot of money.

In 2015, I filed for child support, and when he found out how much he was going to pay, he contested custody in the Attorney General's office. To afford a lawyer, I started working more and more, but I was tired of working weekends and holidays. The hospital owned me. I spent more time at work than at home with my kids. I barely saw my kids. I remember at one point, I was on the edge of my bed crying on the phone to a friend about not wanting to go back to work. Then one day in September, everything changed when a good friend called and showed me this amazing concept. I only had enough money in my bank account for rent that was due in ten days, but I knew that if I didn't do something different, then nothing would change. Knowing that God was placing something very important in my lap, I took a leap of faith, and this concept has been a blessing in our lives ever since.

In June 2016, my ex took my son and refused to return him. When I went to pick my son up, we both called the police. He told the police I assaulted him, but I never put my hands on him. On the contrary, he was the abuser. The police believed him and arrested me, but they couldn't charge me with assault because I never touched him, so they charged me with burglary of my own home. There I was, handcuffed in front of the house I built for my family and my twins in the Honda minivan I bought with my nursing salary. Yet, I had plenty of opportunities to have this man arrested, this man who lied to the officers and had me in handcuffs. Not only was my freedom in jeopardy but so was my nursing license. The same man I put through college for six years was taking away my freedom, my livelihood, and my children all on a lie.

I was treated like an animal in jail and wasn't allowed to use the bathroom for over five hours. I was later transferred to a maximum security prison where women were kept in glass cages. One of them asked me why I was there, and like in the movies, as I answered what my charge was, she finished my sentence. When I asked her how she knew, she said it was because she was in for the same allegation. I found out from her that she had been in for eighteen months, but if convicted, a person could serve two to twenty years. My knees buckled and my heart stopped. I could not believe what I heard. I did absolutely nothing wrong. I prayed harder than I ever prayed before and cried like I had never cried before. But God had a plan. That night, he gave me a vision that I would be reunited with my three children, and I saw us on a beach with blue waters and white sand, laughing and having fun.

I held onto this vision through nearly three years of court dates. I paid 900 to get out of jail, and thirty days after my arrest, my lawyer called and said the District Attorney rejected the case. Although I didn't have to go to court nor report to the board of nursing, the false arrest would still negatively affect me. My ex used this false arrest against me, which ultimately cost me more than my nursing license. The judge took almost all my parental rights away over my son. I was devastated and hurt beyond belief. I had felt no greater pain in my life. I paid five lawyers in total and also had to pay child support for my son even though I was taking care of our twin daughters. I worked almost every day in 2017 and only took off Thanksgiving and Christmas.

In June 2018, my mom called to ask me to move my holiday Tupperware out of her storage. I asked her jokingly if she was moving someone else in, and she said she was foreclosing on her 20-year home. She hadn't been working as she was taking care of my 99-year-old grandmother, whose caregiver of fifteen years had recently quit. I was crushed that my mother was losing her house. I couldn't believe I lost my home to my ex, and my mom lost her home to foreclosure. I swore I would never let anything like this happen again. In September 2018, I moved my mom and my grandmother in with us.

In early January, my friend Johnny called to invite me to a national training event that greatly impacted my life. I started building my business again. I ranked up and started earning residual income, as were my partners. I traveled more in those last six months than I did my whole life. I requested a meeting with my son and the judge accepted because my son wanted to spend more time with me, but my ex denied him that right. The judge finally interviewed my son and I've been granted additional visiting time ever since. I'm glad I never gave up when my friends and family told me I was wasting time and money on trying to get more time with my son.

My mom is one of the greatest women I know. One thing she taught me that you can do anything you want to do. There is nothing that can stop you. God has given us the choice of right or wrong, and faith or doubt. Without God, without faith, I could never conquer the obstacles. I would have never survived my trauma. Ask, Believe, Receive, and Expect it. If I hadn't gone through th trauma I went through, wouldn't have a story to help others conquer their ow obstacles! On many occasions, the following verse has reminded me of my path

"But they that wait upon the LORD shall renew their strength; they shall mount up with wings as eagles; they shall run, and not be weary; they shall walk, and not faint," —Isaiah 40:31 King James Version (KJV).

BIOGRAPHY

Cindy Cavazos has been a Registered Nurse for more than fourteen years i Houston, Texas. She obtained a national Critical Cardiovascular certification an is the single mother of three children, her 20-year old twin daughters, and 17-year-old son. She homeschooled them all their lives, and now the twins a in their second year of college. One twin has a 3.4 GPA and the other twin has 4.0 GPA. Cindy makes over $100k annually. She sacrificed family time and w unable to help family and friends achieve greatness because of her nursing jol In the last four years, Cindy built a small Network Marketing Business that no has a presence in over three countries, and the business growth is allowing her t spend more time with family and friends. She wants to help a billion people an change the world with this concept.

Contact Information
Facebook: https://www.facebook.com/cindy.cavazos.35
Instagram: https://www.instagram.com/p/B1k2SBKBEAK

CHAPTER 10

SELF-IMAGE AND MY IDENTITY

By Devon Kurz

Self-awareness is knowing where I am in life, how I feel about it, what I am doing, and where I am headed. Who I think and believe I am is not as important. It is detrimental to my growth and the impact of presence to believe in who I am not. I must change the way I see myself and have an understanding of my true identity—who I am, the purpose for which I was created—as uncertainty breeds anxiety. This involves understanding who I am, who created me, and what I believe in. Do I believe what the world tells me I am, or do I believe it is my creator? I have struggled with this for the majority of my life...until now. I came to an understanding, a belief, after many years of fighting, pushing my body to its limits, working my life away, and thinking that would get what I wanted as long as I worked hard and long. So, I took twenty-plus years, accomplishing many things except for the things most important in life: family, friends, marriage, and perhaps what is most precious, my beautiful children (Sierra and Conner), who are now young adults. I lost so many precious years and missed out on crucial developments in their lives as they grew up. I didn't see myself as the loving and caring father I wanted to be for my kids. I saw myself as the father who worked, providing money and not time. My identity was

that of a workaholic and not the loving father I desired to be. After all that ha
transpired, I lacked any healthy relationships, I was in poor physical conditio
and health, and I finally came to realize that my life had to be different. I neede
to change, though I didn't have the answer as to how to go about it. I didn't hav
a good mentor in my life—if I did, I wasn't listening, and I never realized it.

One day, a good friend and business acquaintance of mine invited me t
look at something. Dustin said, "Do you have ten minutes to watch this video?
In all honesty, I didn't think I could afford to take the time given all the work
had to get done, but I said, "Sure."

I tell you what—it got my attention and gave me hope. I hadn't felt tha
excited for many years before and maybe ever. I thought that this was the answe
for which I had been looking, and I would finally be able to get my life unde
control. I would have time to spend with those I love and go places with my kid,
family, and friends. I believed that I would do the things I had wanted to do fc
many years.

I was going to be a millionaire—that was what I had told my dad and a ma
(who had come to sell insurance) when I was about sixteen years old. They wer
asking me questions for insurance purposes, and I said, "I don't need insurance–
I'm going to be a millionaire by the time I turn twenty-five." They both looked a
me and chuckled as if to say, "Yeah, right. That's not going to happen."

My heart sank, and my hope vanished for twenty-plus years because I chos
to believe them. They had not done it themselves, nor did they know anyone els
who had done it. When I saw the video Dustin had shared with me, my heart, m
hope, shot up like a rocket! I felt alive again. I was going to do this. I was goin
to change my life. It felt like I had started a new chapter in my life's journey t
fulfill my purpose.

I began to invest in myself more every day, using it as an opportunity t
build a business that would provide for my family and friends. I was excited t
help others achieve what they had hoped to accomplish for years but couldn't fin
that for which they looked. I knew I had something that would have an impac
on thousands of lives and their communities to make a difference in the world.
decided that I would no longer work twelve to sixteen hours a day and seven day
a week including holidays. I was going to travel and enjoy life. I invested som

me into a business a few hours a week. I was making progress, had made a few banks, had received some recognition, and I got back more than I had initially invested. It was a good start. I had never done it before, but I had a team to help me and the support of people who got no direct compensation for helping me. It was unbelievable! I will be honest: it felt good. I was energized by the ability to make a difference in my family's lives and futures. I was able to fit the business into my schedule and add another stream of income without taking away from my construction business. I thought it was great and simple—I could build the business just like I had Decor-N-More—the name of my construction business—by word of mouth. I had the right idea—at least, I thought I did, but it wasn't as easy as I thought it would be. I had started my construction business on a foundation of honesty, integrity, a strong work ethic, outstanding quality, and extreme cleanliness, and it grew by word of mouth. I became very well known for those values and fairly successful in the eyes of others. I believed I could give a repeat performance in the network marketing/direct selling industry.

When I started, it appeared that I would do just that, until I attempted to share my incredible opportunity with two of my best friends, who wouldn't even look at it. I know it wasn't their fault, as I hadn't brought it to them in the proper way. In other words, I didn't follow the system! My heart sank, and my excitement depleted. I wanted it more for them than I wanted it for myself. I felt sick and rejected. I didn't understand why, and I wasn't sure if I wanted to move forward with the business. What was going on? What happened? I no longer had the self-confidence I had with my construction business.

About a year later, a coach of mine, Scott Haug, introduced me to a program called "Thinking into Results" by Bob Proctor and Sandy Gallagher. Scott and his program, "Thinking into Results 2.0," which he had created in conjunction with "Thinking into Results," was instrumental in helping me discover the paradigm shifts in my life. I discovered the answers to many questions, some of which I had yet to ask. My identity is composed of my impressions of who I think I am, but more importantly, who I think I am not. You see, when my friends decided to not look into the business opportunity with which I had presented them, I had taken to heart, as if they had rejected me, and my self-image went back to when I was sixteen and was laughed at because I would never be a millionaire. I had defined

my identity as being a confident construction businessman. I felt secure in wh
I was and what I was doing. I had learned from and worked with my friend
brother, who was very knowledgeable and experienced.

Aaron (a.k.a. Harv) and I had worked together for many years. He ha
mentored and trained me to be knowledgeable in the field of construction, an
the business was known for being reliable and dependable, even though I wa
not known in the direct selling industry, nor was I trusted to be experience
or knowledgeable. I did not identify with the industry as I had in the field c
construction. So, when I had had a few more no's, and I was not able to handl
the emotional impact of the rejection, I shut down.

My hope, my belief in who I was not, was reflected in my self-image an
self-confidence was gone. I began to self-destruct and felt more miserable tha
I can describe. Many areas in my life started to fall apart, though I still studie
the program and continued down the path of personal growth and developmen
I still listened to and attended coaching calls with Scott, but I did not kno
what I should ask to turn things back to moving in a forward direction. I als
stayed connected with my business via leadership calls and events. I bega
taking a "Discipleship Training Institute" class through the Grace Communit
Fellowship—the Church I attended—led by my friend and pastor, Steve. Yo
could honestly say that I genuinely was digging deep, and I was involved. My sel
awareness was growing, and I began to take notice of what seemed to be seekin
my attention—my self-image and how I pictured myself—as Bob Proctor woul
say, "Who I am not."

I don't consider myself religious, even though I was raised under the Church
umbrella. I have come to know and understand my creator. I have always believe
in God, but I didn't follow him, nor did I have an understanding of how to appl
God's word effectively in my life. I didn't identify myself with or understand ho
I had been created in God's image. I am not going to get into great detail—I wi
save that for my next book—but I began to read many of the books in the Bibl
regularly. With an in-depth study of God's word, John writes, "Dear friends, le
us continue to love one another, for love comes from God. Anyone who loves :
a child of God and knows God (1 John 4:7 NLT). In 1 John 5:1 NLT, he write.

Everyone who believes that Jesus is the Christ has become a child of God. And everyone who loves the father loves His children, too."

Through my reading, studying, and listening to my heart and others, I realized that my self-image was not healthy and that I believed "who I was not." I had become someone who I had not intended to be, nor did I want to be. I have always felt as though God was on the outside of me and at a distance. When I realized I was not my true self, I said, enough, and I vowed to change my way of thinking.

I began changing my self-image after I understood from where my true identity came, and with whom I had defined it. In Genesis 1:27 NLT, Moses wrote, "So God created human beings in his own image. In the image of God, he created them; male and female, he created them." In a letter from Paul to the Colossians (Colossians 1:15), he writes, "Christ is the visible image of the invisible God. He existed before anything was created and is supreme over all creation." I accepted my new identity, believing that I was a child of God. I am reminded every morning when the sun rises that I am grateful, and I will listen to who God says I am because He is the one who created me, He loves me, and He created me for greatness for His glory. My life has been transformed since I recognized that my identity had been stolen. More accurately, I had misplaced it, allowing the words of others, who they think or say I am, to define my thoughts.

I discovered what I needed to do. I had to listen to my Heavenly Father, accept and believe in who God says He is, who He is, who He says I am, and who I am becoming. Paul wrote to the Corinthians, "That is why we never give up. Though our bodies are dying, our spirits are being renewed every day" (2 Corinthians 4:16). He wrote to the Ephesians, "Instead, let the Spirit renew your thoughts and attitudes" (Ephesians 4:23). Paul wrote (Romans 12:2-3),

"Don't copy the behavior and customs of this world, but let God transform you into a new person by changing the way you think. Then you will learn to know God's will for you, which is good and pleasing and perfect. Because of the privilege and authority God has given me, I give each of you this warning: Don't think you are better than you really are. Be honest in your evaluation of yourselves, measuring yourselves by the faith God has given us."

My new and true self-image has impacted every area of my life in significant and powerful ways. A mentor of mine, Tony Robbins, said, "Human beings absolutely follow through in who they believe they are. We stay consistent with who we believe we are. We define ourselves. It becomes the glass ceiling that controls us." I agree and believe that we need to be ourselves, the true nature of which we were designed, if we are to progress and produce an abundance in life naturally, and with the effort to raise our standards. We gain momentum through the rituals, disciplines, and intentional habits we put into practice in our daily lives. When we make values and serving others a priority in our lives, our true identities reveal themselves. Our lifestyles should reveal the light and love with which we were created and share it with the world to reveal the light in the world darkness. I like a quote by Leland Val Van De Wall: "Let us not look back in anger, nor forward in fear, but around us in awareness." It is important to stop old conditioning or beliefs that no longer serve from preventing you from becoming everything for which you have been created, are capable of becoming, or earning all you choose to earn. Author Wynn Davis once said, "Every conflict is a set of opposing ideas. All of us have had the feeling of knowing what we should do on the one hand and doing what we feel like doing on the other. By understanding the two opposing forces warring within us, we come to a knowledge of the truth we no longer remain slaves. A clear understanding will make us masters." We must all begin to view conflict and challenges in life as opportunities for growth in our character and spiritual lives. Make it a point to see and remember the importance of your self-image and come to know the power brought about by knowing your true identity.

BIOGRAPHY

Devon Kurz has used personal and spiritual growth for great success in the construction and remodeling industry. He is currently investing time and energy building a business through work ethic and word of mouth. He is excited to serve and help those who are working for and looking to get what they truly want in life. He is excited to lead anyone coachable to the top of their careers. Devon spent over forty years in rural Nebraska. He has two children who are now young adults. He currently resides in Oregon.

Contact Information

Facebook: https://www.facebook.com/devon.kurz

CHAPTER 11

MILK AND HONEY

By Dominika Blum

When I was three-and-a-half-years-old, in November of 1978, my mama and I were at a clinic in Warszawa, Poland, returning a strut device that had been attached to my hips and legs for the previous eighteen months. I had been delivered with forceps and a vacuum due to a complicated birth. I was born with damage to the central nervous system, head deformation, hydrocephalus, stretched sternoclavicular and mammary muscle, hypertrophic pyloric stenosis, and hip dysplasia. The hospital released me as a child from the "risk" group because there was nothing they could do for me.

Nowadays, doctors recognize such conditions and have x-rays readily available if needed. Back then, in communist Poland, one could wait up to three months to do a simple x-ray. Doctors did not want to give referrals to see specialists as they believed their own knowledge would suffice. Thank God, my mom was determined to heal her baby. We traveled all over Warsaw on a bus to find experts who would help so she could get me the aid critical to my wellbeing. Though she went through hell and back in the first few years of my life, she didn't give up. She was the one who taught me determination and resilience, and for that, I will be forever grateful.

After we returned the leg braces, we had to get my three-year-old leg muscles strong again. Mama got me a tricycle so I could ride around our tiny apartment to exercise those little legs. As my body got stronger, I went from tricycling to walking, running, and dancing like no one was watching. I sang, and I danced everywhere you could imagine. Mama signed me up for all types of dance classes at our city's Dom Kultury (House of Culture). Since then, dancing is one of my favorite things to do, and I often dance in my kitchen or anywhere, really. The feeling of great rhythm flowing through your veins is one of the best things in the world, and it's an invigorating mood changer, too. Spiritual teacher Eckhart Tolle believes, "Life is the dancer and you are the dance." I couldn't agree more.

Eleven years later, on May 3, 1989, riding in a yellow cab from O'Hare airport to Jefferson Park was a ride I will always remember. Everything was so big. The cars were long and wide. The highway had so many lanes, and the taxi driver spoke in a funny language I did not understand. Everything looked so different, so alive and fresh. The air smelled of limitless possibilities. Because of my Polish American stepdad, we moved to Chicago, Illinois. The United States of America. The greatest country in the world. The country of milk and honey, the land of the free, where everything is possible.

I was excited about the move, curious about the unknown, and eager to embark on this new journey. I knew it would be hard, but I did not expect it to be as hard as it turned out to be. Late nights of studying became the norm, as did learning a new language, memorizing the words, the grammar, the slang, and the "in-words." Learning and understanding the United States Constitution and history to fulfill my eighth-grade requirements without being fluent in English was challenging. The Internet and online language courses did not exist at the time. There were no smartphones and no apps to teach word pronunciation. treasured the daily disciplines my mom taught me as a child. The belief that could learn a new language, that I could achieve greatness, grew stronger. I had no other choice. If it was meant to be, it was up to me.

The first year in my new world was one of the hardest in my life. I cried myself to sleep most nights, but to thrive and not just survive, I had to rise above it—rise above being made fun of and bullied at school, rise above my cruel school mates. Rise above it all. We have to persevere to succeed in life. One of those successes was when I earned 97% out of 100% on my US Constitution exam.

Success. /sək'ses/ Noun, the accomplishment of an aim or purpose. To succeed, one has to know exactly where one is going, have a clear vision, put in a continuous effort, believe in yourself, do the right thing, be consistent, have grit, be grateful, and, most importantly, love what you do. When you love what you do you will not work a day in your life. Success starts with daily habits and discipline. The only place success is found before "work" is in the dictionary. We can't expect to succeed if we don't put in the work.

My mentor taught me to win the day, every day. Every day do what you can control. Do not worry about or waste your time on anything else. Just focus on what you can do right now. Focus on what you can do today. Ask yourself, what can you do right now to start achieving the goals you have in your heart. Start with the end result in mind, see the prize, and pay the price to get what you want. Envision exactly where you are going, have a plan, and work that plan. Make decisions based on faith and not fear. Henry Ford once said, "Whether you think you can, or you think you can't, you're right;" do your part, and God will do His.

After high school, the question wasn't if I would be going to college, but which college I would go to. I went to one of the best universities in the nation for my major, and I graduated with honors and a Bachelor of Architecture Degree. One year later, I realized that being an architect was not what I wanted to do with the rest of my life. I wanted to change lives. I wanted to travel the world and embrace all of the life experiences I could. I did not want to be stuck in a traditional nine-to-five, and I started to look for a way out. I answered an ad in the paper with the headline, "Airline Attitude!" I had found it. I was so excited! This was my first introduction to working in sales, which was a highly competitive and flexible environment, and I loved it. I loved helping people. I loved the numbers game. I loved the pursuit. I loved the excitement of it all.

My work was based on commission pay only, and not all months were as lucrative as the one before. I started waiting tables part-time as another stream of income while I figured out the sales game. Man, oh, man—did I get an earful of OPO (other people's opinions). Note to self: never listen to anyone who does not have what you want—this applies to all aspects of life—relationships, money, health, wealth, lifestyle, education, experiences, and the like. If we buy someone's opinion, most likely we will end up buying their lifestyle. According to experts, the average toddler hears the words "no," "don't," or "can't" four hundred times day on average. It's no wonder we don't always believe in our own abilities, as w are trained our whole life not to.

I was twenty-five-years-old, and for the first time in my life, I was introduce to the idea of personal development. "What do you mean we have to work on ou minds?" I asked my mentor. The concept was so foreign to me. I then realized tha I already had everything I needed to succeed. I had the control to make my lif what I wanted it to be, and it all started with what I fed my mind. I began to rea good books like *Think and Grow Rich* by Napoleon Hill, *The Magic of Thinkir Big* by David Joseph Schwartz, *The Power of Positive Thinking* by Norman Vincer Peale, and *The Power of Your Subconscious Mind* by Dr. Joseph Murphy, to name few. I nourished my mind with positivity through good books, CDs, workshop seminars, affirmations, positive self-talk—whatever I could get my hands on— every single day. Our brains are like gardens—what we feed our minds matte What we focus on expands. Ask yourself, are you feeding the flowers or the weec in your mind's garden.

Over the last twenty years, I have invested a lot of time, energy, and mone in my personal growth. The best investment one can make is in one's self, after al We all need to work on ourselves every day. Just like taking a shower or a batł we need it daily. Work on your mind muscles daily. This is a lifelong process. Th minute we think we know everything there is to know, we go right back to wher we started. Be intentional with who you include in your circle. We have the choic to surround ourselves with positive, loving, driven, goal-oriented people who wi uplift us and push us to be and do better, believe in us, and tell us the truth. W must seek out action-takers, powerhouses, go-getters, leaders, achievers, doer. kind, selfless people with huge hearts. I choose to learn and broaden my horizor on a daily basis, using that knowledge in my life. I don't believe that knowledg is power; I believe that knowledge combined with action is power. We can b the most educated people in the world, but if we do not do anything with tha knowledge, it does not matter how much we know. To get what we want in lifu we must ask for what we want and not what we don't want. Most importantl what we want must be backed up with love and action.

Ralph Waldo Emerson once said, "The only person you are destined to become is the person you decide to be." Every experience makes us stronger and wiser and drives us to make the right choices. 2012 was a year of major life decisions for me. I resolved to cut myself off from friendships, relationships, habits, and behaviors that did not serve me positively, and I found my purpose. I love exploring and traveling the world. My mom is my biggest inspiration in this area, as she's the one who got me hooked on traveling and discovering the world when I was little. Travel humbles us by showing us how little space we occupy in the world. It teaches us in the most profound ways, stretching our way of thinking, our beliefs, and our imaginations. Saint Augustine of Hippo described this idea when he said, "The world is a book and those who do not travel read only page." Creating memories with friends and loved ones across God's earth has an impact that will live in us forever. I have traveled to forty countries and thirty US states so far, creating a life from which I do not need a vacation. I am committed to reading the whole book and taking a bunch of people with me along the way.

One must serve others from the heart and see the world from a place of love if one is to be successful and feel fulfilled. The more we love, the more we get love back. Love is a purpose. It is our true power. It is what inspires us and what changes us. Love is at the core of success. Love is the key to all. "We love because He first loved us," 1 John 4:19. God first loved us, so love yourself just the way you are. Love one another, speak life, not death, into your daily life and trust God to do His work. He has a grand plan for all of us. A part of God's plan for me was to serve in Guatemala. I volunteered at San Martin municipal for the first time in 2015 with the Hug It Forward organization that helps build schools from plastic bottles filled with trash. I immediately fell in love with the culture, the beautiful people, children and their love for one another. The El Chocolate community stole my heart and changed my life forever with their big hearts and warm smiles. I returned to Guatemala three more times and led volunteers from across the world to build bottle schools. I am stoked to go back this year for the fifth time in my life, this time with college students from a local university. I look forward to watching them grow into servant-leaders on this volunteer voyage.

Our attitude and mindset, showing up, being present in the moment, and having the belief that you will win are all a part of victory's bigger picture. My good friend, Roscoe, says that you've got to show up and participate in your own rescue. We all live in a time of abundance, but when we make decisions based on fear, we believe the lie that we live in scarcity rather than abundance. Whatever we believe becomes our truth, turning our perceptions into our realities. Our words are powerful. We speak life or death into our lives daily by what comes out of our mouths. We either build ourselves up or tear ourselves down. It is so easy to be negative, to complain and play the victim. I challenge you to change your way of thinking over the next thirty days and start paying attention to your thoughts and words. When negative thoughts manifest, change them to positive ones. Love instead of hate. Think before speaking. Compliment instead of complaining. Be the victor God made you to be. There is more than enough love, abundance, prosperity, wealth, and goodness in this world for everyone. God gave us dreams and goals for a reason. He sent us into this world not to be in it, but to transform it.

My purpose and mission are to help millions live their best lives. By aligning our actions with our intentions, we can make our dreams come true. It does not matter where we come from. It matters where we are going. Begin by writing down your goals and affirmations and read them daily. Visualize what you want to do and be. Start from a place of love. Believe in yourself, practice positive self-talk, and take massive action. Relentlessly persevere daily, no matter the circumstance. Though it sounds cliché, don't sweat the small stuff. Do your part, and God will do His. Dream BIG and go after it. Get your milk and honey, friend. You are worth it.

BIOGRAPHY

Dominika Blum is a sought-after leader with a vibrant and contagious attitude. Best known for her laughter and servant leadership. She is a passionate entrepreneur, speaker, and international advocate for education. Dominika has been inspiring people to live their best lives for the last twenty years. Her mission is to transform millions of people by helping them rise to their highest potential. She believes everyone with the right attitude and mentorship can achieve their goals. Dominika is a life-lover, travel fanatic, dream-pursuer, and relationship-builder. When she's not traveling, you can find her encouraging others, learning, and reading. Her guilty pleasure is ice cream and romantic comedies. She is married to the love of her life, John, the best husband ever. They live happily in South Dakota, USA.

Contact Information

Facebook: https://www.facebook.com/sunattitude

Facebook blog: https://www.facebook.com/UwierzwSiebieDominikazWarszawy

Instagram: https://www.instagram.com/sunattitude

Twitter: https://twitter.com/sunattitude

LinkedIn: https://www.linkedin.com/in/dominika-blum-53046a19

Email: dominikablum@gmail.com

CHAPTER 12

THE MAGIC OF LIVING OUTSIDE YOUR COMFORT ZONE

By Helen Kithinji

I am backstage, surrounded by media production machines and the production team. In the background, I can hear loud hip hop music that sounds like a million people singing along. The auditorium is electric. This extravaganza is making me even more nervous, just as one of the media guys is fixing my mic to go on stage. This is my first time ever hosting an international event. This one is a three-day business training event in Johannesburg, with over 4,000 entrepreneurs from all over Africa in attendance. After my mic is fixed, I ask the production director to give me a couple of minutes to calm my nerves. He didn't need to know that I was going to pray and then telephone my coach. My heart was racing, my palms sweating, all of which was reminding me of a past experience in a similar situation.

I was assigned the role of introducing my singing group during one of our performances at the Conservatoire in Nairobi, back in my high school days. Our music coach Mr. Walshaw had prepped me well. Once on stage, I was to take one step forward from the other 11 singers, introduce the group, then give an outline of the classical pieces that we were going to perform. I'd spent two weeks memorizing my short speech and practicing every step, the pose, and the smile. I had mixed feelings, as we waited for our performance slot. I was feeling excited about the opportunity, yet nervous and scared at the same time. When our time came, we walked onto the stage, formed a neat semi-circle, while the audience applauded. When the applause was over, our music coach signaled me to start. I stepped forward to do the introduction. I could barely see the face of the audience through the dim lights, but I could feel their eyes on me. The pin-drop silence paralyzed my mind and my mouth. I went blank. I couldn't remember what I was supposed to do or say. I stood there tongue-tied, trembling, staring into the audience like a statue. That one minute felt like five minutes and only ended when Mr. Warshal snapped his fingers from the far end of the stage. Everything streamed back into my mind, and, judging by the applause after my speech, I had done a good job, after all.

The memory of this experience gave me a tremendous fear of public speaking for a long time afterwards. Indeed, when I was working as a public relations manager in the bank where I worked many years later, history repeated itself during a bank-customer relationship event. My boss missed his flight, and had to host the event. When I stood on stage to kick off the event, my mind went blank again. I remember the sweaty palms, my heart racing, and my whole body trembling. After a minute of paralysis, I gathered my courage and managed to run the day's program smoothly. This was the last incidence of my stage paralysis but definitely not the last of my stage fright. Over the years, I have had numerous occasions to speak onstage, every time experiencing nervousness and anxiety, especially in the minutes just before going onstage. Today, I no longer have those mind-locks and am more relaxed on stage. Taking training courses on how to be an effective speaker and practicing every time I speak means that I get better each time.

You would think that having spoken onstage many times before, I would be confident about hosting my first international event. After all, the only difference here was the size of the stage, the audience, and the auditorium. I had prepared well, carefully choosing my outfits, accessories, and my hairdo, and I'd practiced my opening speech, researched some stage jokes, and watched videos about

mceeing. But here I was, deathly nervous, almost about to back out at the last
minute. But my determination to be a highly sought-after speaker got the better
f me. I spoke to my coach, who guided me through a centering process. I took
ome deep breaths, whispered a prayer, and was finally ready to face my fear. As
my name was announced, I walked onto the stage, raised my hands up in the air,
inviting the audience to stand and dance with me. As I danced across the stage,
my stage fright was suppressed. My courage was boosted by the love and energy of
the audience. The audience danced along happily, with some people shouting my
name and sending flying kisses, fueling my courage and strength. I had interacted
with most of the people in the audience in person or through social media. Most
had been following my journey, as I built my global travel business, becoming a
top thought-leader, and earning a million dollars in commissions over six years in
our part-time, home-based business. It is my success in this business that earned
me the coveted chance to host this event. My journey to earning a million dollars
, one I can summarize in one sentence: "I found my fortune outside my comfort
one." I've found that my growth always comes from pushing myself through
uncomfortable experiences.

When I look back at my early years growing up and then as a young
professional, I've found that my major achievements were always preceded by
intense fear, anxiety, and the temptation to quit. As human beings, we're inclined
to try to protect ourselves from the unfamiliar. We tend to resist that which pushes
us out of our comfort zone and toward change. Yet it's through change that we
grow.

All personal breakthroughs begin with a change in beliefs. That's what I've
earned over the years; to make a breakthrough in our personal development, we
have to start by challenging our long-held beliefs that were formed during our
upbringing and our life experiences. During my early years, my beliefs about
success were shaped by my parents and the community around us. For instance,
my father was a traditionalist who believed that one only needed to work hard in
school and get good grades to secure the ideal—a job with the government. The
most coveted government jobs at the time were high-school teacher and district
administrative officer because they were seen to provide job security and a modest
salary to live on until retirement at sixty.

My observations told me that the majority of civil servants lived peaceful average, event-free lives, providing the basics for their families, but never really achieving massive success. Because I had bigger dreams for my life, I decided to focus on securing a job with a multinational company or a bank. My father and his generation grew up with the belief that working for the government presented the best opportunities and that it was difficult, almost impossible, to qualify for job in a private enterprise. After making applications to fifty-three banks listed in the yellow pages of an old directory, I secured a position with the largest bank in the region. Fifteen years later, I exited the banking industry as a highly successful senior bank executive to become an entrepreneur.

Ten years have passed since then, and I have grown into a successful entrepreneur. I run a global business, have invested in a couple of other businesses including a financial institution, where I serve on the board. I've achieved accreditation for executive coaching and often publicly speak to and train entrepreneurs. I'd like to share the key principles and lessons that I've employed to create a system for continuous growth in all areas of my life, including my health and fitness, parenting, relationships, career, business, lifestyle, and spirituality. Most recently, I achieved the milestone of having earned a million dollars in my home-based business in only five years, an achievement that I never thought was possible.

1. **Identifying and replacing limiting beliefs**

    Personal development and my coaching training exposed me to the power of questioning every limiting belief that stands in my way of achieving my goals. Psychologists have proved that our brains are always trying to move us away from anything unfamiliar or that we think might cause us pain. By asking powerful questions to interrogate such beliefs, you can overcome and replace them with supporting ones. Some of the questions I ask are:

    "How has this belief served me in the past?"
    "How has it limited me in the past?"
    "What will it cost me in the future if I don't act against this belief?'
    "What more empowering belief can I replace it with?"

82

It's time to get rid of beliefs that do not serve you! Make a list right now, ask the questions, and then commit to replacing them with empowering ones.

You'll no doubt find that limitations will also come in the form of justifiable reasons or excuses. These, too, must be subjected to the same process outlined above. For example, in the past, I told myself that I couldn't go to the gym because I didn't have time. After going through the questioning process, I realized that neglecting my fitness would cost me later in life in the form of medical bills. I dropped the excuses and hit the gym.

2. **Setting high standards**

To create intense desire and drive to achieve audacious goals, I set high standards for myself. During my banking days, my boss was always astonished at the aggressive targets that I set for myself. This practice saw me ascend in my career faster than my peers. I continue to use this principle in my businesses and personal projects.

3. **Commitment to continuous learning and personal growth**

Your ability to expand your mind and commit to lifelong learning is critical to your success. My commitment has seen me get ahead in every aspect of my life. There are three forms of learning, namely; *Maintenance Learning* aimed at keeping you in your current position; *Growth Learning* to increase your skills and knowledge, and lastly, *Transformational Learning*, which contradicts and challenges your beliefs, triggers new insights, and creativity to move you forward beyond that which you believed was possible. You can continue the learning journey through certified training events, online courses, books, and validated content.

All successful people that I know of commit to continuous learning, with most reading at least a book every month. Consider the extreme reading habits of billionaire Warren Buffet, who is reported to read fifty books a year and spends hours reading hundreds of pages of business reports every day. Could this routine be one of the keys to his massive success?

In Japan, they have a continuous improvement system called Kaizer So, based on my experience and knowledge, I recommend committin yourself to the habit of constant and never-ending learning for growtl This is an investment in yourself that will enrich and enhance you relationships, families, businesses, and communities.

4. **Working with a mentor**

Finding the right mentor to work with can propel you on your way t success, allowing you to be guided by someone with superior experienc and knowledge of your chosen field. It's an effective way of shortening th learning curve and avoiding unnecessary mistakes. Your mentor will hel you to challenge any beliefs you hold that may be blocking your way t success and boost your self-confidence, leading to further breakthrough Throughout my life, my mentors have played an important part i supporting and cheering me. They've celebrated my achievements whe I've been successful; and supported me through tough times, helping m to understand my limiting beliefs and pushing me to overcome them.

5. **Discipline yourself to take action consistently and persistently**

One of my mentors has always said that success doesn't come easily c quickly, you need to be patient with the results but impatient with takin the right action to take you forward.

My message is: Consciously and consistently push yourself outside your comfo zone in order to continue a positive progression. Learn to notice when your belie are limiting you and replace them with empowering ones. Imagine that they ar the brick wall that you must crash through to achieve your dreams. Don't le the fear of failure stop you. Overcome the fear by doing what you fear anywa If you're willing to do what is uncomfortable for you to move yourself in th direction of your ambitions and have the courage to tackle the unfamiliar, eve when you have no guarantees for success, you will ultimately succeed. It's part c the process to allow yourself to learn through failure, and trust that every time yo ll, you'll get up having learned a lesson that puts you closer to achieving your oals. As Thomas J. Watson, former CEO of IBM, put it, the formula for success simple— double your rate of failure.

Living outside your comfort zone will bring you heightened levels of nergy, passion, and an enduring state of happiness and satisfaction. It is simply 1AGICAL!

BIOGRAPHY

Ielen Kithinji is a successful entrepreneur, investor, an Accredited Executive Coach, and author of one of the most powerful personal development books ublished: *Profiles on Success with Helen Kithinji*, which also features other global est-selling authors. An MBA graduate, her story about growing to executive nanagement in her fifteen-year banking career, becoming an entrepreneur, and stablishing a multi-million-dollar global business in less than five years continues provide inspiration and encouragement to others in pursuit of their dreams. he has been featured in leading business publications, including the Voyager Magazine, Business Daily, The Daily Nation, Business for Home, and The tandard newspaper. She has won several awards, her latest recognition being the chievement of a million dollars in sales commissions in her online business. She lso enjoys a rich, happy family life with her husband—Ronnie—and their two dorable sons.

Contact Information
acebook: https://www.facebook.com/rahalinks
nstagram: https://www.instagram.com/helenkithinji/
Website: https://www.helenkithinji.com/

CHAPTER 13

I CHOOSE ME

By Ilioara Ormenisan

Why do human beings give up on things so easily? Has this question ever come to your mind?

My entire life, I've been seeing people around me give up easily on their dreams and goals. Since I realized that, I've been wondering why that is, why don't they want more for themselves. I can't be the only crazy person wishing for things that may seem unachievable.

I've been surrounded by people saying that they want more money and fulfillment in their lives. Yet, when opportunities come, they seem to be blind to them. It's almost as if they're putting on a blindfold and embracing NO with ease, instead of making more positive choices.

Looking from the outside, we can see that people are usually capable of doing what they want, but they just don't see it.

A while back, I was one of those people asking what my purpose in life is. Sometimes, I'd get frustrated, as I bought into other people's ideas about what life should be. Back then, when I wondered about this, I thought of all the many things I know how to do, like baking, sewing, decorating, handmaking crafts, cleaning, ironing, nail technician, etc. But none of that felt like my true mission in life.

I found myself making negative judgments about myself and thinking i
the same downbeat way. I felt similar to the way I did before my husband and
started our relationship. We've known each other for 26 years, but our romanti
relationship only started seven years ago. Before we started hanging out, I wa
single for two-and-a-half-years, and every date I went on was a failure. Plus, a
the time, I had the feeling that everything was falling apart. At one point, whe
I thought about this, I remember thinking that I was sure what was "mine" wa
waiting for me, but wondering when I was going to find it. I often felt the sam
about my purpose in life, too.

After all this destructive self-talk, I realized that I wasn't heading in th
right direction and needed to start looking at things from a different perspective
What if, for instance, my mission in life was to be happy, spread happiness an
joy around me? That could lead to amazing situations. I started to enjoy th
little things in life more and began to see the good in people, even the ones wh
annoyed me. But the most important change I made was to start being mor
grateful for everything around me—and I mean, absolutely everything.

Have you ever been in a situation where you felt it was right to trust you
gut about something and, despite anyone else's arguments, you went ahead an
did it anyway?

I surprised myself by acting this way even when my family and friend
disagreed with my intentions. But I knew I had to trust myself and take that lea
of faith in order to move forward. It wasn't always easy. I have been blessed wit
challenges, but my intuition has usually proved that I've made the right decisior
You might wonder why I say I have been *blessed* with *challenges?* Let me explair
By deciding to change my outlook, I came to the conclusion that every challeng
(I stopped calling them problems long ago) I faced in my life could be overcom
if I faced it with courage.

I believe this has helped me become a better and stronger person toda
I hope you understand the message I'm trying to get across—that challenge
are actually *blessings* in disguise. It's not so much about the challenges that w
encounter throughout life. It's about how we face them and deal with them.

I am 100 percent certain that every single one of you, at some point i
your lives, have come across a situation which, at the time, left you breathle
or completely stressed out. Then, after tackling the issue, you looked back an

ought that it wasn't really that bad after all. I'm not sure how true this statistic really is, but it certainly feels as though one percent of life is what happens to you and 99% is how you react to it.

Please allow me to share my story with you: I always considered myself an ambitious person, but kind and sweet at the same time. Although I saw myself as a fighter in life, committed to succeeding, and working hard to achieve my goals, I still gave up on things from time to time, which led me to the question we started out with. For a long time, I couldn't find an answer to that question of why we sometimes quit things we've started. Maybe I wasn't thinking about it hard enough? Besides, I could always blame it on human nature—that this is who we are as people, and that we are capable of changing our decisions overnight. Have you ever felt this way, or is it really only me? I don't think so.

People might call me crazy and a dreamer, but I believe in magic, and no one in this life or the next can shake my opinion on that. I always considered myself as having a special something, but never really knew what it was. But now feel that I do.

Do you know that feeling when people are trying to force you into choosing between two different options? That's not me. I'm not the type of person who makes those kinds of choices. That's not my reality. I'm talking about choices that have a long-term effect on you, like quitting college, a relationship, or giving up on a dream that others say is crazy. Isn't it better not to buy into their points of view, but do what you feel is right? I remember a situation that happened before went to university: I was in a dead-end situation but couldn't accept it. I had choice between going to university or staying in a relationship. But I didn't want to choose—I wanted both. What happened was that, by not choosing, as most people would, the challenge of having to find ways to overcome obstacles to having both sent my brain to work. And it came up with solutions that worked. This just proves my point that, when you ask yourself questions, your mind is forced to answer.

I'd like to share another story from a few years ago about this point of view: three months after I got married, I took the decision to leave my family, my home country, and move abroad without my husband. The reason I did that was because I wanted us to own our own home. To achieve that, we needed money for

BREAKTHROUGH SUCCESS

the deposit. So, I emigrated to the UK to find a job and save up the money for it. If I'd let my family's arguments against going influence myself, I would have stayed at home. But I was determined to follow my instincts that it was the right thing to do, and I would succeed in my aim. Sometimes, thinking logically about something just gets in your way. I thought about the fact that I was going into the unknown, I hadn't even got a job in the UK, but I dismissed any worries.

Instead, I listened to my heart, which told me to proceed with my plan and follow my dream. Now, it sounds so easy when I write about it, but at the time I remember having days when I felt like the sky was falling in. I had it planned that I'd work for six months, save all the money I could, then go home. Except that, in the beginning, I was told that we needed 5% of the total mortgage cost, but when my husband checked six months later, the realtor suddenly wanted 20% and gave us a one-week deadline to find it or lose the house. Once again, I set my brain to work and looked for solutions to the challenge. This is another example of the approach I take with all challenges. I never accept NO for an answer when it's something I really care about.

The important point I'm making here is that I knew what I wanted and fully committed myself to achieve it. I chose to believe in myself and my gut feeling that my choice was right.

I've realized that when I choose to commit to my deepest and, some might say, unacceptable desires, dreams, or goals, which I believe in with every molecule of my body, other people's opinions can't sway me. When you're committed to yourself, you will never give up doing what you think is right, because that conviction comes from inside you. It comes from the heart, and no one can stop that burning desire. Do you remember hearing stories about mothers saving their children from death by almost superhuman effort? From somewhere, they find the strength to save their child, even if it means lifting a car or breaking thick window glass. The same thing happens with us when we're functioning in that space where we feel our dream, our purpose coursing through every single part of our body. It's your life that we are talking about. It's not something to be treated as a New Year's resolution that you give up on after a few days, weeks, or months.

When you truly decide to commit to yourself, when you take charge of your own life, then it's not important how many followers you might have, it

90

bout knowing where you're heading, following your gut instinct, going with our intuition. You have to trust, have faith, and certitude that, when the time is ght, you will succeed in your goals because you know your purpose.

Throughout our lives, we let ourselves be influenced by so many people, y family members, by doctrines, but who's to say that they're right and you're rong? We tend to be judgmental about our actions and often feel guilty about ur decisions. We live life doubting if we've made the right choice. But, what if ou can choose to create new and different possibilities? Please, would you do me huge favor? Could you stop living other people's lives and start living your own, 1 the way your soul truly desires? Don't let yourself be overwhelmed by all this, 1st take the reins of your life, even if it means breaking out of your comfort zone.

Right now, you might be thinking, *"Pfft! I already live the life I want."* But ; that true?

If that's you, then you're not lying to me, you're lying to yourself. Let me ive you a tip about choosing—did you know that you can choose to change your eality every ten seconds?

I encourage you from the bottom of my heart to take a few minutes for ourself and take a retrospective look at your life; think about the things from the iture you can bring to the present; ask yourself how you really want to live. You an even write down a list of the changes you desire to make in your life. Now is he time to erase all negativity and stop postponing things: It's time to CHOOSE 'OU and take control of your life.

BIOGRAPHY

Ilioara Ormenisan is an ambitious, caring, and hardworking entrepreneur. She ; creative, persevering, and passionate about traveling. She has a strong desire to nake an impact on the world. Her mission in life is to spread happiness, hope, nd joy around the world by encouraging others to follow their heart's desires.

Contact Information
Facebook: https://www.facebook.com/ilioaraormenisan
Instagram: https://www.instagram.com/ilioara/

CHAPTER 14

SEVEN LIVING GENERATIONS

By Ilze Strauta

At present, seven living generations span across the planet. These generations are seven distinct groups of people born within a defined period who shared similar cultural traits, values, preferences as they ged, and therefore have similar ideals.

Different countries have different generational definitions based on major ultural, political, and economic influences; however, here are general cultural enerations.

910–1925: The Greatest Generation
926–1945: Traditionalists or the Silent Generation
946–1964: **Baby Boomers**
965–1979: **Generation X**
980–1995: **Millennials or Generation Y**
996–2009: Generation Z
010–Present: New Silent Generation or Generation A

hough it is easy to fall into overly generalized stereotypes when talking about generational differences but each generation's future is affected by its childhood the outcomes of different childhoods are similar to the experiences and outcome of history and the future. Every generation has a set of needs, values, and dreams However, historically each generation holds some bias against another.

People in different countries were influenced by different events, politic and social life. Due to rapid technological evolution in some countries, peopl could accomplish and cultivate culture and social life faster than in other countrie It is all the more crucial to consider the characteristic differences of all generation as today at least four to five working generations are part of the labor market working together under one roof. This century faces an unprecedented challenge that is, to prevent misunderstandings between generations, which could lead t unnecessary conflicts. Sooner we understand what drives different generation sooner we find a way to interact with each other.

How do we find a common language?
Pay attention to the signs of conflicts, controversies, and needless blowouts.

The Greatest Generation

Shortly after World War I, this generation witnessed a new era—stuck betwee childhood and reality of the war—called Depression Era. The war led to the deat of millions of people, destroyed long-established peace and economic stability, an created conflicts between many countries in Europe, Middle East, Russia, Asi and Australia. This generation became compulsive savers, careful with spendin money, and felt responsible to leave a legacy. They grew up to be patriotic an authority-abiding citizens.

The greatest generation lived without the aid of technological advances, lik airplanes, radio, TV, refrigerators, electricity, and air conditioning. The concep of "retirement" was alien to them; you worked until you are dead or cannot wor anymore. Divorce was a taboo, and relationships were forged for eternity.

This generation experienced not only technological and medicinal chang but also a huge culture change.

Traditionalists

Postwar, this generation was surrounded by darkness, doubts, and everlasting concern, but it was at the helm of new work and business opportunities.

Peace, jobs, suburbs, television, rock 'n roll, cars, Playboy magazine, and the Korean and Vietnam War—were few of the defining moments for this generation. Women stayed at home, looked after children, and waited for their husbands to come back from work with a hot dinner. While men worked for one employer their whole lives and provided security and comfort for their families, this generational believed family to be a sacred and eternal entity (meant to be together forever), while children born out of wedlock were not accepted by society.

This generation earned and learned to save money. They planned for retirement, to make up for the hard life after the war. They have been financially prudent, the richest, most free-spending retirees in history.

Baby Boomers

Born after the war, baby boomers are part of the generation when the attitudes, behaviors, and society, in general, were rapidly changing. They were born to work, to be employees, and to be careful and patient. They are very loyal and reliable.

In Europe, after World Warr II, the society experienced a postwar economic rise. In Russia, people underwent various side effects of socialism and collectivization. The United Kingdom faced an economic crisis. In the United States, while many people served in the military, the country's economy was still in better shape. With the advent of industrialization, manual production shifted to machine production, and manufacturing companies provided jobs. Baby boomers worked to secure their children's lives.

Self-righteous and self-centered—too busy for neighborly duties yet strong desires to reset and change the common values for the good of all—this generation became workaholic. Baby boomers are liberal and modest; they were not a part of the labor market but were loyal to one employer their whole lives. They are well-suited to be a team player and oriented toward collaborations. Working with one employer your whole life was considered to be honorable.

Baby Boomers' spending habits and consumerism fuelled world economie
They became famous for spending all the money they earned. Spend now, worr
later, buy it now, and use credit— they are not adept with finances. After the wa
several planes were converted into passenger planes, which enabled Baby boome
to travel and experience and see more than their parents ever did.

Generation X

Acquiring education and climbing the career ladder are important for Generatio
X. They look for opportunities, are result-oriented, and focus on self-developmer
and independence in their private lives and financial matters. Not only are the
profit-oriented, but they also love to work and live for themselves. In profession
spheres, Gen X is motivated by recognition, trust, career advancements, an
financial rewards. Followed by baby boomers, they learned to find a balanc
between theory and practice. They witnessed the fall of the Berlin Wall, the collaps
of the Soviet Union, spent most Saturday nights at a disco, MTV, microwav
ovens, color televisions, video games, and personal computers.

Often called ''lackey kids,'' both their parents worked. Consequently, th
generation is typically independent and does not thrive on micromanagement, an
can even be considered entrepreneurial. They focus on saving the neighborhooc
instead of the world. They are tech pioneers because they saw the transition fror
the industrial to the digital age and had personal computers, microwave oven
and video games at their disposal.

Gen X is not the core advocate of the government. They suffered from th
increasing drug problems in schools, mindlessly used credit cards, craved hig
status in the society, and blindly chased money.

This group desires to achieve a higher quality of life and prefers lifelon
learning and earning opportunities.

Generation Y

This generation experienced the 9/11 terrorist attack, internet era, cable televisior
satellite radio, 2008 financial crisis, the extreme effects of climate change, Googl
Skype, PayPal, Facebook, and so on.

Pursuing passion and following interest in work took precedence for this generation. They accept difficult tasks as a challenge and are not too loyal to the employer. They want to work for themselves, and they regularly change jobs to gain financial advancements. They prefer to work in a team, expects leisure time, and can be confident yet aggressive. Growing up at the beginning of the technological globalization, they know everything about everything.

They are ambitious and have a flexible work schedule and an interesting life. They expect regular feedback from their managers, and if they feel unappreciated, they don't shy away from changing jobs.

They grew up as skeptics, but they are energetic, go-getters, and have leadership instincts with built-in self-confidence. With the technological advantage and great digital skills, Generation Y refrains from participating in a "rat race" but works hard like all previous generations. Work-life balance is important for this generation as most of them came from unhappy, divorced families, and saw their parents working two jobs.

Generation Z

Generation Z seeks freedom and self-awareness. They believe in the joys of work and leading a happy life. They carve their lives around the 24/7 principle. They expect challenge and trust at work; are realistic and individualistic. Workplace safety is important for this generation. They are self-starters, confident, and value-oriented. They are known to find new ways to make money and gain fame and profits rather efficiently. They are fascinated by dynamism and are prime multitaskers.

YouTube has come to aid for this generation. They are realistic and understand that no employee can become a millionaire. They learned early in life that time is precious. They are not afraid to take responsibilities or be in leading positions, but they separate private and work life. Gen Z is uncompromising when it comes to working on weekends.

At present, Generation Z occupies a small part of the labor market, but they are very technologically oriented, fast learners, and adapt quickly. They are accurate and creative and eager to be financially stable. They harvest information off the internet.

Their lives are built around and blended in smart devices, modern technology, internet, social media, Facebook, WhatsApp, etc. They are adept in online business techniques, like email marketing. However, their self-worth is often based on the "likes" received on social media, which makes them sensitive to criticism.

However, they appreciate working with experienced colleagues. As most of them still are students, and only the future will show what to expect from Generation Z.

Generation A

Generation A or "digital babies" are exposed to advanced technology from birth. They are born in a fast-changing world with an abundance of information. They are technologically literate from birth and would be experienced in the use of touch-sensitive or artificial intelligence-enabled devices.

Although some parents might be against allowing their children to use technology or limit its usage, such restrictions are of little benefit. Most schools are rushing to transform their teaching methods and incorporate digital technology. It might seem like a clip from a dystopian movie, but this world is the new reality where the new generation is dependent on technology.

Perhaps in the future, Generation A will realize the power of human interaction and the need for emotional attachment.

Bottom Line

Age is just a number, and technology advancements are part of our lives. I am looking forward to more development leading to more exciting opportunities.

If we shut ourselves to new possibilities and don't want to understand and accept changes, the conflict will be knocking on our doors. Had we followed "New way is not a right way," or "Nobody has done it before," humanity would not have progressed. The invention of the light bulb was not a touch of the devil but the persistence of mankind toward a major advancement of the civilization.

The amalgamation of the work of all generations has led us here. Everyone's work is meaningful, and for that, we must be grateful to each other. Everybody xpects a decent salary; a leader who listens and respects their point of view; ipport from others; and to lead a stress-free life. This is the basic expectation, ot a stereotype.

Every generation brings in this world their own set of values and views, iotivations, and attitudes. Different people and generations make life interesting. o, do not let life escape from you.

BIOGRAPHY

ize Strauta has studied psychology, marketing, entrepreneurship, restaurant ianagement, art, and history of art in Latvia and Russia. She has learned, iastered, and practiced network marketing, social media and digital marketing, nd business in the United Kingdom, Europe, and the USA. Strauta worked n hospitality for twenty-four years, before venturing into writing. She has xperimented with several occupations: secretary, restaurant manager, event ianager, human resource manager, brand host manager, and regional training ianager. She considers mentoring and coaching people, who struggle to step p, her favorite passion. Strauta loves to travel, explore different cultures, local uisines, and meet interesting people. She believes that her Latvian sense of humor as helped her to overcome the challenges of life gracefully.

Contact Information
acebook: https://www.facebook.com/life.travel.success
nstagram: https://www.instagram.com/life.travel.success/

CHAPTER 15

ACHIEVE WHAT YOU WANT

By Iréne Wrigstedt

M y story is my legacy to my children and grandchildren. I hope it will give them the courage to believe in themselves, follow their dreams, and achieve what they want in life.

I want to encourage people who face challenges and think that they lack the ability to dream big.

Everything is possible. Don't let negative thoughts limit you and don't listen to negative people. Determine what you want, express it, and embrace it courageously when it shows up. Go with your gut; it knows what's right for you.

I always have dreams. I am not afraid to fail. The goal can always be amended.

It's not that I don't listen to other people—I used to do it a lot and followed what they said even if I didn't agree. I stayed quiet to avoid conflicts.

I grew up as a lonely child with loving parents. I was their everything, which turned out to be a significant burden. Everything should look good. My father once told me I was *a good average person.* It has followed me to date. I developed a self-image of not being good or intelligent enough. I imbibed it and lived the first part of my life in the shadow of that perception.

Even though it felt lonely to grow up without siblings but not having anyone to lean on or get help from has made me strong.

Due to the experiences growing up, I made it a priority to be kind, loving and caring toward others. I try to support and help my children and friends as much as I can.

I value honesty, love, trustworthiness, and ethics. As long as you are brave and have faith, success will follow.

I always did things outside the box even before I knew the expression existed. People often laughed at me and criticized me. I think it says more about their insecurity than about me.

Money and creativity drives me. Growing up, I experienced a lack of money; my parents were open with me about our financial condition, which made me anxious. Later in my life, being totally broke taught me the value of money. It became my goal to build financial security for my children and me.

Creativity is also an important factor. I love nurturing ideas and developing them into businesses and help people grow.

When I was twenty, I moved to Lausanne to work. My parents repeatedly warned me that it would not be possible to find a job and a place to live. But I was determined. I had been studying there after the gymnasium and had a great time studying, partying, and skiing. I moved, got a job, a flat, and continued the fun life.

After two years, I was ready to move back home. I wanted to buy a horse. Ever since I was little, I was horseback riding, so it was a long-due wish. Due to the cost involved, my parents did not support me, but I had saved enough to buy a horse.

Even though they did not support me initially, my parents did not shy away from boasting about me coping so well in Switzerland and back home my participation in horseback riding in front of their friends. That did hurt me as they did not support me from the beginning.

I was raised as a good family girl, always conditioned to do the right thing. I was trained in how to *behave* in various situations. I did not understand why it was important and of what use. Despite all this, I did my own things.

All this amounted to making me feel prestigeless, which I see both as good and bad. Good because I don't care about prestigious things, and I am not afraid of being embarrassed. Bad in a sense that people might perceive me as having no courage or impact.

Being prestigeless does not mean that I don't own prestigeful things such as nice clothes, nice cars, and a beautiful house. I have decided to indulge in these luxuries for my pleasure and happiness, not to gain validation from others. I am not boastful, just grateful though I have experienced jealousy, which came as a surprise to me.

I have never been jealous. I take full responsibility for my actions and for what I have achieved, and I am happy for other people achieving success.

I was asked to go in therapy by my husband and my business partner to become more easy to manage. So I did.

I also did some massive life coaching at Landmark—making up with your past and creating your future. It changed me as I gained insights about myself and was given tools to make changes if I wanted.

I asked for a divorce from both my business partner and my husband.

After moving back from Switzerland, I started working as a secretary to the CEO, something my parents had encouraged me to do. I served coffee, took shorthand, typed out letters, and behaved kindly. I performed well, but my bosses were still unhappy as they could not *master* me. So, I took a degree in marketing and started a new career.

In 1992, I saw an opportunity to set up a business based on a concept that did not yet exist in Sweden. The timing was right, and the market was there; I hit the ground running. I also brought in a business partner. After a few years, I expanded the business to Denmark, Norway, and Finland. I had seventeen offices in four countries with around three-thousand people on the payroll.

As I was still living with the self-image of *a good average person*, I did not assert complete authority in my business. I relied on my business partner too much, who prohibited me from talking to our staff because I did not do it the right way, and they were afraid of me. I believe that it was my business partner who was afraid of my success.

While in the business, I gave too much authority to the senior manager, which resulted in me losing control of the company.

At a turnover of a hundred million Swedish crowns, I filed for bankruptcy in four countries due to the lack of control. I also found out that people whom trusted had cheated me.

I ended up broke. I had built a big company, helped my clients earn a lot of money, and given my employees good salaries as I appreciated their work. Everything fell apart in a few days, and no one had anything good to say about me. I was left with absolutely nothing.

As my clients were well-known, the media in four countries started to chase me to dig scandals and sell stories about me. There was nothing to find, but they were dealing with a naive person with a lack of control, so they started to concoct stories. It was an awful experience.

Despite the downfall, the business idea was still fresh, and the market was still responsive. A businessman saw this as an opportunity and stepped in to earn money. I was very vulnerable and did not object as he put a good plan into action. He decided everything and I just followed. For me, it was good. We reopened in Sweden and I moved to London to continue the business I already had there. After a few years, our partnership came to a bitter end and we sold the business.

This gave me some money, and I went on doing what I always thought was cool—living on a beach in a beautiful sunny place. I moved to Barbados and started a Jet Ski rental business. I soon realized that life on the beach was the same as in an office and had similar problems.

So when the person with whom I was testing a business idea in France six months ago called and informed me that our client wanted to roll out and wondered from where I intended to work. I realized I needed to go back and pursue the business that I was good at. Luckily, I spoke French.

I spent ten years in France, and we built up a big company. We designed our own offices—a 750 square meter wooden building with central heating and rainwater harvesting system. A wooden, ecological building led to a lot of media coverage.

After being away from Sweden for fifteen years, I wanted to move back. missed my children and grandchildren. So, I sold my part of the company.

It might seem like that everything has been easy, but that's not the case.

Almost everything I have done received criticism. I often ask myself where got the courage to go after what I want, bearing in mind the people who tried to top me. I think I am naive. I express what I want. I do not see the obstacles, or if see them, I do not let them decide my course.

For instance, when I moved from the outskirts of Stockholm into the city, I anted to live on the street where my mother grew up because I have nice memories f my childhood with my mother and grandparents. I wanted an apartment there ith a terrace. This street has old buildings with no terraces. People told me that would never get one. I found my apartment with an eighteen-square-meter rrace.

Another time when I lived in London, I wanted to live by the sea. I had ved by the sea for a short period in Barbados, but I wanted the same in Europe. just did not know where and when.

I met with my French business partner at a convention in Paris. He saw my pecific skills and asked me to set up a company with him. He lived in northern rance by the sea. So my flat happened to be just a few meters from the sea.

While moving back to Sweden, I decided to live in the village where I spent y summer holidays ever since I was a one-year-old girl and I have many pleasant emories. I wanted a land by the lake. But there was no land to buy by the lake. did not exist. I was determined and kept expressing my desire, and after a while, e real estate agency called and showed me a land—by the lake.

I designed my own house with an indoor swimming pool that has always en my dream. I received several negative comments about how difficult it is to ave an indoor swimming pool. Ironically, from people who never had one.

Today, I live in a nice house by the lake, and I own my dream car—a ercedes convertible. I have a dog—a lovely five-year-old Rhodesian Ridgeback— at I always wanted, gifted by my son.

I am grateful for what I have. I have it because I have been brave. I have ways expressed what I wanted. I have not let the negativity affect me nor listened the naysayers.

I have gone through difficult times, filed for bankruptcy, two divorce raised two children on my own, and an ex-husband who committed suicid These challenges never stopped me.

I now look forward to my new career in the network marketing busines which is a new experience for me. When I moved back to Sweden, I wanted t learn something new, meet with new people, and undergo new experiences.

A friend introduced me to the possibility of earning money in a new an exciting way by leading, cooperating, and helping other people to succeed togethe with me. I have just started this exciting journey, and I am determined to succeed

Here is my advice:

- believe in yourself
- do what you want to do
- follow your gut feeling
- don't seek all answers in the beginning; eventually, they will show up
- don't be afraid of failing
- be brave and take opportunities as they come
- don't pay heed to negative people
- don't believe everything you see on social media
- base your decisions on your own experiences
- don't harbor preconceived opinions; look for facts
- be kind, helpful, honest, ethical, loyal, trustworthy, and loving
- be persistent—it takes time to build something stable

It is not always easy, but I keep working on my life every day.

BIOGRAPHY

Iréne Wrigstedt is determined, stubborn, and does not mind the obstacles, which has led to achieving her goals. Iréne wants to encourage others to dream big—express your goals, believe in yourself, be brave, and you will get what you want. She writes about life experiences and the consequences of her decisions and actions. Iréne has been a self-employed entrepreneur for thirty years. She introduced new market ideas, built companies in six European countries, had thousands of employees, and helped hundreds of clients to make money. She has made mistakes and failed. But this didn't stop her, and she continued working on new projects. Iréne lives in Sweden. She has two children and grandchildren who are precious to her. She loves her long daily walks with Khathu, her lovely Rhodesian Ridgeback. She plans for a new career in network marketing, along with playing more golf and dancing more salsa.

CHAPTER 16

REACH

By Joan Kenyon-Woods

From my humble beginnings in Jamaica, West Indies, I understood the concept of hard work. As a five-year-old child, I remember caring for my aunt's and uncle's children. I had chores, too, like fetching water from a huge well. There was always the possibility of falling in and drowning, but that thought never crossed my mind because I was given the task of fetching the water for cooking or washing, and I had to complete it. Young, old, everyone became adept at gathering water from that well. Being expected to contribute along with everybody else taught me the value of family, community, hard work, and what takes to succeed.

We left the idyllic countryside of Jamaica and immigrated to England when I was about six years old. I was enrolled in school, which was not such an ordeal, as I was already accustomed to the British education system that the Jamaican schools had adopted. However, I was not prepared for the class that was placed in—I was in the third class from the bottom. It was a system that packed students into homogeneous groups. The school was called Copland, and the classes corresponded to the name, with C being the highest and D the lowest. was placed in A, the third from the bottom. As I languished in that class, I was acutely aware that I did not belong there. I felt smothered and lost. My constant thought was that there had to be more than this. I knew I had more in me, and wanted more. I suppose I manifested what happened next.

I loved sports and excelled in track and field. I always gave my all and was very competitive. I could run faster than some of the boys in my school. The British love sports, and track and field is popular. I ran track, and I also played game called Netball that is the female equivalent to basketball, except you can move once you have the ball, but only pivot. The objective is the same—you score by getting the ball through a netted hoop. I loved sports because it created a level playing field for me. What I seemed to lack in the classroom, I made up for on the sports field.

For my parents, being in class 7-A, the third from the bottom, meant failure. Like Sisyphus, it seemed that I was rolling the stone of my high school life up a hill destined to have it roll back down into this dead-end of a class. However belief and a great attitude can change everything.

It was sports day; my time to shine! It rained—that's England, but I was determined that it was not going to rain on my parade. I had a positive attitude and upbeat spirit, though I do not know where it came from. Although, I have to say, my parents were happy people. My dad always made jokes and wanted people to laugh, and my mom loved to laugh.

That sport's day, the gym teacher left the playing field and casually said, "Joan, you are in charge," as teachers did in those days. Nowadays, you dare not leave a class or students to their own devices. It is a recipe for disaster. But, that day, something switched on inside me, like a light bulb coming on. I rallied my team, and we took on the biggest and the toughest.

Although, the tough kids were not going to succumb to the authority of another kid. So, it was a scrappy game. My nemesis, who shall remain nameless, dropped the ball, which I promptly kicked—only to have it hit her right in the face. To say that I thought I was dead meat is an understatement. I had one recourse, she had to catch me first. I didn't have time to think, I just started to run. I knew neither she nor anyone else could catch me. And she didn't. That the first and last time I ran from a fight. I don't mean a fistfight, hell, I'll run from those every day, but I decided at that moment that I would face life's challenge head-on.

Not long after that, the same teacher—my savior, my mentor, my hero—
moved me from class 7-A to 7-C. The challenges of this elevation in life were
many. Now, I was required to work twice as hard to get the desired result. The
greatest reward, however, was the caliber of people with whom I was now rubbing
shoulders. It was as though my whole life had turned around in an instant. I do
not remember the people in class 7-A, but, to this day, I have lasting friendships
with many of the people in 7-C. What did I learn? I learned about discipline,
persistence, and perseverance. My mind expanded and never contracted again. I
developed an avid interest in personal development, consuming as many books
as I could on the subject; I realized that the world is wide, and I wanted to know
how wide. It was not as though everything changed overnight; it took some time
to adjust. But adjust I did. I wasn't good at math, so I was in the class below,
7-O. It mattered not. When I was with the movers and shakers, I leveled up. I
elevated my thinking, my expectations, and my efforts. The conversations we
had, the ideas we discussed, It was as if I was part of a mastermind group. We still
have those earth-shattering discussions about politics, relationships, religion, and
everything else.

These were brilliant people who I did not know existed until my gym
teacher changed my circumstances, for which I will be eternally grateful. I often
think of Mrs. Okupa and have tried, in vain, to find her. I remember those little,
short, all-white outfits she used to wear, like a tennis player. They were crisp
and clean, with precise and well-formed pleats. That was her uniform, and she
wore it every day. It seemed as though she must have had hundreds of the same
outfit stashed in her wardrobe. I don't remember what part of the continent she
originally hailed from, but her African accent was rich and warm, and she exuded
confidence that commanded respect. She was loved by all, but perhaps most of
all, by me, because she was responsible for transforming my life and putting me
on the path I was to follow. It was Mrs. Okupa who gave me the belief in myself
that I have relied on all my life.

Then one night, when I was writing this book and talking to a friend, my
phone began ringing. It kept on incessantly, but I didn't answer it—I had that
sinking feeling, the one you get when the phone rings late at night—it must be
bad news. However, when my aunt, who lives in Canada, and my cousin, who

is usually asleep by 8 pm, kept on ringing, I knew it must be something seriou. When I finally plucked up the courage to answer, it was to learn the news I ha been dreading; my beautiful, lively, generous, intelligent, hard-working mothe was dead. Alzheimer's is a cruel disease, and she had been suffering from it for while. The whole family was forced to watch, appalled, as this wonderful woma literally deteriorated in front of us. Of course, despite knowing her death wa likely to happen at any time, I was devastated by the news, and the loss was sti very painful.

However, as time passed, my initial sense of panic gave way to th remembrance of all the wonderful lessons she had instilled in me. I remembere when I languished in that dead-end class, my mom always encouraged me t reach a little further, do a bit more, and aim to be more than I was. When I thin of my mother, I think only of her successes. I knew there had been failures i her life because my parents were divorced, something which my mother nev really got over. However, I also watched her turn that failure, as she saw it, int a resounding success. She was, by all accounts, a workaholic. That was why m mom ended up owning four houses within ten years of us moving to the USA. was through lessons such as these that she taught me to reach for what I wanted

When we immigrated to the United States of America, the move cou have been far more traumatic than it was, if not for my mom. We had to leav everything behind in London: my dad, my friends, my way of life, even boyfriend. But my mom made the transition easier, taking us to live with m aunt, who had us all working within two months after our arrival. We arrived i September, and by November, I was working in Macy's, New York. That was culture shock. We were all living my mom's dream. I would hear her talk on th telephone to my aunt back in London, who told my mom that the USA wou give her everything she wanted—and she was right.

The job at Macy's famous department store was my first ever—and turne out to be quite an important one for me. To get there, I had to travel int Manhattan every day on a crowded, smelly, hot train without having a clue ho to navigate my way through an equally crowded Manhattan. I worked in th lingerie department, and enjoyed selling the most expensive nightgowns, those couldn't afford, to the many husbands and businessmen who asked my opinio was difficult getting up in the morning when it was bitingly cold, but I did it because I knew that my salary helped support our household, and none of us could live for free. I was grateful for the strangers who sometimes gave me their seat on the crowded train. It didn't happen often, but when it did, I was genuinely grateful.

In retail, the adage is that the customer is always right. I don't know if the customer is always right, but I do know that you should always be polite towards them at all times. Customers might often seem annoying, irritating, demanding, and sometimes ridiculous, but, in serving them, we must make a conscious decision to respond positively and be as helpful as possible. Although there are times when we would like to give way to our emotions in such circumstances, it's better to remember that the moment we lose control, we have lost control of the situation.

In retail, one learns to practice mindfulness. The ability to control one's response to external events becomes almost a part of one's DNA and can be the key to success or failure. One has to reach inside oneself and regulate one's emotions, and have some compassion and empathy for oneself. By developing this ability, one gradually learns to decrease the reactivity and mood fluctuations that can occur when one lets events trigger and control one's responses.

One practice that has governed my life is remembering to be grateful. Be grateful for the little and the big things. I remember an old proverb, I don't recall the exact words, but the message was: "Gratefulness can transform the common days into thanksgiving; it has the power to transform life's routine tasks into joyful ones and turn opportunities into blessings." As the author Robert Brault advises, enjoy the small things today because, one day, you may look back and realize they were the big things.

Human beings have an infinite capacity for greatness, so what is it that causes us to fear reaching out for that greatness within us? Is it simply that we fear rejection, the knock-backs, or the ridicule of others? As Franklin D. Roosevelt said, "There is nothing to fear but fear itself." But how does one overcome fear? I think it is simply by taking action to do the thing that one fears. Yes, that is how one overcomes the fear. Let me share an example with you from my own life: I was on a trip to some exotic part of the world and was offered a ziplining activity that consisted of three levels of ziplining. I was eager to have a go, but there was a young lady who had accepted the challenge but, at the eleventh hour, became fearful. I was incredulous, as she was already at the top of the fifty or more steps that we had to climb. There were people of all ages there. I was one of the oldest and there was a young boy of about ten among the group, too.

I began to talk to this young lady and discovered it was her birthday, which is why I assumed she had taken the trip. Now, she found herself fifty feet in the air, ready to zipline across the jungle. She cringed and held back until the last moment. I shared with the group that it was her birthday, and we began to sing Happy Birthday to her. This completely changed her mood— there is something magical about that song. She smiled and laughed while I gently coaxed her into the harness, and she was made to feel secure. I assured her that I would not leave her and even held her hand. Then, before we could exchange another word, she was whisked off over the jungle. I met her at the next level; there were no more jitters or fear in her eyes. Everyone who had arrived before us cheered and clapped for her and, yes, we sang the birthday song again.

BIOGRAPHY

Joan Kenyon-Woods is a motivational speaker, entrepreneur, and world traveler who exudes positivity. Joan has utilized her professions—as a teacher for sixteen years and a social worker for more than a decade—to gain insights into social and emotional responses to life's varied hills and valleys. Joan was a member of the National Speakers Association, where she rubbed shoulders with the likes of Zig Ziglar and other well-known motivational speakers. A wife for over thirty years and a mother of three, Joan is not only a successful businesswoman but also a loyal friend.

Contact Information
Facebook: http://facebook.com/JoanKenyonWoods
Instagram: https://www.instagram.com/JKWoods_love/

CHAPTER 17

UNLEASH YOUR POWER WITHIN

By Josef Buchmayr

A ustrians are different. At least that's what people tell me when talking about business. I don't believe it. In my experience, people all over the world have the same dreams, desires, and aspirations with one thing in common—time. Everyone has the same 24 hours a day. It is how we treat these hours that makes all the difference.

Let me tell you how everything started for me. As a young boy, I had big plans. If someone asked me then, what I would like to become as an adult, my answer was straight forward: "I will become a millionaire!" My perspective has changed a lot since then. Today, it's no longer just about creating wealth for myself and my family, but to help others in living life on their terms. To be able to do so, for most individuals, includes having the benefit of time and money.

Most people either have one or none of the two. So how do you get both time and money at the same time? You need to own a business. I'm not talking about being self-employed with no employees—doing all the work on your own. I'm talking about being a business owner and having a system that works even if you're not present.

The moment you find a system that works for you and make the decisio to pursue that path, your subconsciousness or inner programming needs to b fixed to unleash your power, live up to your maximum potential, and fulfill you wildest dreams.

You have to recognize that you're worth it, and it is okay to live a life c abundance and have more than those around you who weren't willing to persi and pay the price. You don't have to feel bad or have a guilty conscience if you g the success you always dreamed of.

Let me tell you my story. Even though I had big dreams as a kid, I burie them. Only because a person very close to me told me that it was impossible t become a millionaire if you didn't have your first million dollars in your ban account by the early age of eighteen. As a young boy, this seemed out of reac to me, and that's why I listened to my parents and chose the academic path t prepare myself for a good job.

When I was nineteen, I had my first encounter with entrepreneurship. M father introduced me to two businessmen who showed me a venture they wer working on. That day, I envisioned a limitless future and got so excited that couldn't sleep. I began working, but facing the first few challenges, my enthusias wavered, and I quit.

I don't recall exactly, but about one or two years later, a good friend of mir called me and pulled me right back in. We worked on a business venture togeth and had some initial success. Not long after that, things got tough, and my frien decided to no longer partner with me. This was during our student days. Th time I didn't quit, but I stopped putting in the effort necessary to advance on business and got back to student life. Indeed, it was not much different fro quitting.

After receiving a master's degree in Business, I decided not to wo for someone else, but to live the entrepreneurial life again. The timing wasr perfect, as the industry I picked was telecommunication with a focus on landli telephony. I worked hard to establish a business, but the product was going out the market rather than flourishing. Considering the wrong timing, it didn't tal long until I ran out of money and had to get a corporate job. I felt devastated an depressed. I lost faith in myself and felt worthless.

Looking back at my career and the several setbacks I have faced so far, have realized one thing. The greatest enemy of your success is you. It's your subconsciousness sabotaging your efforts. It's your subconsciously thinking that you cannot be more or have more. It's you subconsciously telling yourself that money is hard to be made and that success is something for people better than you. It's your subconsciously believing that you don't deserve the success you're striving for. This is what held me back for so long. When you finally let go is the time when everything will suddenly come together and move in the right direction.

God has a sense of humor. A couple of years later, after I had established myself at a big international company and started earning a decent income, entrepreneurship showed up at my doorstep again. I met with an old friend of mine whom I hadn't seen in a very long time. He mentioned a business idea that he was now pursuing. This is when I pulled myself up and started a new venture. Only this time while working in a demanding job and having a young family to take care of. I believe God wants to test you and see your true character before he lows the universe to be on your side.

But what should you do if you find yourself in a situation with very little time for a new business? I will give you five steps you can follow.

Step 1: Have a Vision

If you have a good and well-paid job, your family and friends won't understand. Most people, including the ones closest to you, don't believe that an affluent life is possible for them, so why should it be for you (even if you have their best interest in mind). In the beginning, they won't support you, or even worse, they will be against you working on your business. To endure and become successful under such circumstances, you must have thick skin. And for that, you need a *vision*. You have to see the future before everyone else does. You must envision a bright future and imagine all the good that will come with it, for you, your family, friends, and all those you influenced.

Step 2: Make Time

As I mentioned earlier, everyone has 24 hours each day, not a minute more or less. So if time is a constant, how do you make time? The truth is, with the decision to do something new, something old has to go. If you're still spending time watching TV, playing video games, or consuming gossip and negative news, these are things you can easily reduce or get rid of completely. Besides that, you can evaluate the work that needs to be done on a regular basis, like household chores or gardening. You could hire someone to do these chores for you.

If, after that, you still need more time, these are the sacrifices that come along with your decision. Family time and hanging out with friends may have to go as well. You must not neglect your friends (your real ones) and especially, your significant other and children. You have to reach an understanding that is okay for everybody. I, for example, made an agreement with my family that Sundays are family days, which means no work from dawn to dusk on Sundays—*family only*. So if occasionally I have to make a conference call on a Sunday, I have to ask permission first. And if a family trip is planned on that day, the call has to be rescheduled.

One tip here: Open up your mind. Instead of telling yourself that it isn't possible to get any more time, ask yourself, how is it possible? This way, your brain will go to work for you and come up with some ideas. You might be able to squeeze in a call on your commute, or you can meet with somebody during your lunch break.

Step 3: Find the Right Things to Do

Now, as you've found a couple of hours every week that you can devote to your business, you shouldn't waste this time. You must work efficiently on getting things done in these hours as humanly possible. This means no distractions and laser-focused work. But just working efficiently doesn't get you your desired results. You also have to pay attention to the tasks you are performing during these hours. In every field of business, there are a handful of tasks you have to do to achieve results; these are often called income-producing activities. Find out the venture-specific tasks and focus solely on one of these during the precious time you have for your business.

Step 4: Create New Habits

Successful people have one common characteristic: they do the things that average people don't. They don't necessarily like every task they do, but if it is necessary for them to achieve their goals, the temporary pain is well worth the payoff that they've visualized in their minds and are soon to experience in reality.

Whether you like the task or not, to do something you're not used to requires willpower, and this will bring down your overall energy level. If you don't like a specific task, it will require even more willpower and drain your energy faster. There is good news. You can relax here. Push yourself to do the activity for ninety consecutive days, every day without fail, and you will create a new habit. After this period, it will even feel awkward if you don't do the activity even for a single day. But don't try to establish too many new habits at once. Pick one habit at a time; otherwise, it might get too overwhelming, and you might give up before the activity turns into a habit.

Step 5: Persist

Work hard and don't look left or right for at least one year. Have faith that despite all possible difficulties, hurdles, and setbacks along your way, you are on the right path, and everything will turn out fine in the end. Keep on going until the success is yours.

Let me conclude with this: we're all on a journey, and we always will be. And because we are more powerful than we believe, it is our duty to always get better and to march forward and make a difference in the world. So if you ever feel overwhelmed, read this fantastic quote and know—*you're worth it!*

Our greatest fear is not that we are inadequate. Our deepest fear is that we are powerful beyond measure. It is our light, not our darkness that most frightens us. We ask ourselves, who am I to be brilliant, gorgeous, talented, fabulous? Actually, who are you not to be? Your playing small does not serve the world. We were born to manifest the glory of God that is within us. And as we let our own light shine, we unconsciously give other people permission to do the same."

by Marianne Williamson

BIOGRAPHY

Josef Buchmayr holds a master's degree in Business from IMC Krems, a renowne University of Applied Sciences in Austria. He spent time abroad in Polan and the Dominican Republic. He now works for a big international compar headquartered in Vienna, being responsible for risk management in Canada an the USA. Besides that, he is building a business in the travel industry and enjo helping people to live a life full of fun, freedom, and fulfillment. He loves t spend time with his five-year-old daughter and his one-year-old son.

Contact Information
Facebook: https://www.facebook.com/TripleF.sunshine/
Email: buchmayr.marketing@gmail.com

CHAPTER 18

THE POWER OF FAITH

By Leslie Freeman-Wright

Scotland's national poet Robert "Rabbi" Burns famously wrote a poem— *To a Mouse*, in which he wrote the immortal words (translated from the original Scottish): "The best laid plans of mice and men often go awry." These lines are often quoted even today, perhaps because they contain an eternal truth—even our most meticulously laid plans and schemes are often disrupted— by unforeseen things that happen in our lives. Just when you think you've thought of every detail, drawn up a brilliant, fail-safe plan, and set reminders for yourself, somehow that "thing" you'd set your mind on ends up falling through the cracks. When our carefully laid plans come crashing down around our ears, we often feel that all we want to do is run away, maybe to a quiet beach, where we can forget everything and just listen to the waves crashing on the beach while we drift off into *Neverland*.

That feeling is something I completely relate to. In the early part of 2018, I felt everything I'd worked for, along with my marriage, my faith, and my family were slipping away from me. I had no idea what to do and nowhere to escape to; I was lost. Not knowing or understanding how I was doing it, I woke up every day and went through the motions. At the time, I felt as if I was in some sort of coma, standing back and watching my life crash and burn like a downed aircraft. I felt powerless to act in the face of unforeseen life events.

It began when my father passed in July 2018. Within hours of his passing I landed a whopping six-day period of hospitalization from a disease I'd never even heard of. As a result, I couldn't attend my own father's funeral. As you can imagine, I was devastated. Life as I knew it was already a whirlwind, but suddenly not having Dad around felt as though everything inside me was dead. Those of you who have lost a loved one will understand this feeling. At the same time, I realized that my marriage was failing, and felt there was no one to turn to share the burden. I was in a complete daze. Just like most people going through such events, I began to realize just how precious and short life is.

Prior to this, I had dreams and aspirations of becoming "someone." Back then, I didn't understand that I was already "someone." I had to dig deep inside myself to find the strength, the motivation, and faith in God's will to make it through the days. Fortunately, my husband and I realized we wanted to save our marriage and make it stronger. We discussed it and decided that we'd create an entirely new marriage. We both understood that no one's perfect, and that we needed to regroup and go back to the time when we initially said "I do" to each other. Part of the problem was that we both have such busy schedules, but we knew we had to work out a way forward and make a decision. That decision was to *work at working* on our marriage. At that point, it was like God tapped on my shoulder and gave me the tools that we needed to rebuild our life together. It wasn't easy, but it was worth it.

You see, I realized that I was placing my faith in all the wrong areas at first. By definition, faith is having complete confidence and trust in someone or something. When I looked closer at my life, I saw that all along, I'd been hoping for different outcomes in most areas of my life, but somehow expected them to occur miraculously, without any effort on my part. I wasn't putting in the work and effort to make the changes necessary to bring about those wished-for outcomes. Instead, I questioned why things, both good and bad, were happening but never took the time to take a step back and try to understand the reasons for them. However, there came a moment when I finally slowed down and took a breath; that pause gave me the chance to see that everything happening was more significant than me and that I alone wasn't going to be able to change it. For once, I had to make myself believe that I wasn't a terrible person and that my marriage

asn't failing. That horrible feeling of being in freefall, that everything you think
ou have a hold on is disintegrating, might actually relate to things falling into
lace. By looking at things from a different perspective, I began to understand
hat the trials and tribulations I was going through might actually be in my favor.
Hard to believe, isn't it? This is when the phrase "with God all things are possible"
ame to mind, which helped me to understand that the faith factor I was missing
was ME. I'd given up on me a long time ago, and it took my world to fall apart
or me to look up and see that I believed in God and his faith in me, but I needed
o rebuild myself and my faith within if I was going to move forward.

When I sit back and look at every major obstacle that was thrown in my
direction during that dark time, I now see it as a period of preparation: Preparation
or what was to come and finding the way to getting where I wanted to go. I
elieve that all things happen for a reason, and light shines on every shadow;
m here to testify that believing in myself and what I could do with passion and
ositivity set forth in my life, and a change of mindset is powerful.

With this new insight, I fought for my marriage; I went to individual and
oint counseling with my husband. Together we created a prayer wall, read a lot
f relationship guide books, and went to a marriage retreat. There we learned
aluable life lessons that not only helped with our relationship but also to become
he positive role models our two beautiful girls needed. Talk about relationship
oals! I'm proud to say that through our fight, determination, efforts, and hard
ork, we are now one hell of a power couple, and I'm so glad our kids have strong
ole models to look up to.

Life wasn't easy, and trying to rebuild it from the ground up was a definite
truggle at times. There were tears, yelling, breakdowns and the "give up" attitude.
fell victim to that situation where you wake up every day wondering what else
as going to happen. Many times, I just wanted to close the chapter and walk
way. I wondered how things had got here, where did we go wrong? Yet, at the
ame time, I had to dig deep, stand still, take a deep breath, and start the day
new, and keep pushing on to find the belief that I'd buried deep inside. One
f my sanctuaries was going to my fathers' gravesite. There were days when I'd
ist park my car alongside the cemetery and cry while playing some of Dad's
vorite music. Though he wasn't physically here on earth, he was still there for

me. Anytime something new happened in life, good or bad, I'd make a point of going to hang out with him, make sure he was okay, and share my stories with him. Of course, even today, it still breaks my heart that I wasn't able to attend his funeral because I'm sick with a disability that's invisible to the naked eye.

At times I felt angry, questioning God as to why these things were happening to me, asking where did this disease I'm afflicted with come from, and why now. I'm not going to lie; that was by far the most difficult part of my grieving, not being there for my dad. However, as with all things, I know he wouldn't stand for me, NOT getting the proper treatment that I needed. Yes, all of this was going at once, and good days were hard to come by.

But, through these struggles, I somehow managed to find out what a strong person I am. I might have been broken, or so I thought, but I never let that keep me down. Somehow, through the pain and the sadness, I mustered the energy to pull through. I believe staying in tune with myself and the new version of who I wanted to be made all the difference. I refused to let the bad win. I'm a fighter and I would prevail. Aside from my past and things I couldn't change, I could still learn from what was happening. I learned from my mistakes, so I knew what NOT to do moving forward. I had to fix my mindset and remain as positive as absolutely could. My energy spilled over into my relationship, and my husband and I began to implement changes, putting into action everything we'd learned over the years, so that our love began to thrive once again. I could have walked away numerous times, but that is the easy way out. Easy for the relationship, but hard for the kids affected by their parents splitting. But again, learning to fight for what you believe in, and letting faith intervene was the blessing that I needed.

What would you do in time of need? Would you take the easy route and walk away, or would you stay and work for a better lifestyle? Would making changes to your daily habits benefit your overall health, both physically and mentally? If they would, how bad would changing your mindset, life, and routines be if you knew the outcome would be beneficial? What if you had no idea what was on the other side? Would you make the leap of faith and believe in yourself to see what the outcome would be?

Everyone has a story, a struggle, a romance, a heartbreak, but not everyone is strong enough to pull through them. Life has a sense of humor where you find et the test, then the lesson comes later. It's kind of crazy how that works. What ou don't realize is that everything seems important—until you get sick, whether at's physically or mentally. For it's at such times that you realize what's really nportant to you. Believing in your self helps you to find a way to keep going and build your life, to leave behind whatever has you stuck.

Most importantly, you'll learn to take care of your health and start to realize at whatever you were fighting against might be the very thing you need to work n to make it right. Sometimes, you just need a moment to exhale, take a good ook in the mirror, and realize what you have and what you're working with. If ou alter just one thing every day, you'll see what God can do. Believe in yourself, ecause the power of faith is so strong. If you just believe in yourself, as I learned do, and alter one thing at a time, your mindset will change, too. My experience roves that all great things happen to those who work hard for them and focus on elieving that faith lies within themselves.

To date, my husband is my rock, my confidant, and my best friend. We en't perfect, but the Lord knows we were meant to be joined as one. Together, e're working towards our future goals and building a proud legacy that our girls n one day emulate. It's all about the right mindset, belief, and faith. You don't ave to believe in God. Just remember, if you don't have faith in yourself as a erson, then no one else will. There are times in life when you just know that ou have to do what your heart tells you, when you decide to take a chance on lfilling your longheld dreams, even if no one else can see that. Going through ese tough times taught me that the power to take control of my own destiny as in my hands— I had a vision, and I didn't want to lose it. Time after time, I ced seemingly insurmountable odds and stumbled, but I reminded myself that m in charge of my own destiny, I am a mother to two young girls who need a rong role model, a wise leader, and supporter. If I wasn't healthy both mentally d physically within my relationship, then I was a failure, something that I never anted to be. I knew that if I didn't make changes and uplift myself to find my wn happiness, then I couldn't expect those around me to look at me as a source f strength and positive motivation. We all fall, but it's up to you and the faith you ave inside you, to choose whether or not you get up, and how you do it.

BIOGRAPHY

Army Brat turned Army Wife, Leslie Freeman-Wright, tells the story of her li
and her journey to becoming an important role model for her family, as well
in her community. Working for the airlines, Leslie travels to many places fo
training events, learning, and teaching others about the industry and how t
become successful. In addition, Leslie has been an entrepreneur for over ten year
stepping out into the world away from her day job, and experiencing other thing
that life has to offer. She has always wanted to write her own books, and finall
found her niche through training others to find their full potential in life. B
doing so, she has found happiness by helping others succeed in everything the
want and love to do. Leslie has also been an advocate speaker at several trainin
seminars and continues to lead everyone she meets find happiness and success.

Contact Information
Facebook: https://www.facebook.com/leslie.freemanwright
Instagram: https://www.instagram.com/poison3f98/

CHAPTER 19

HOW MOMS CAN CHANGE LIVES AND IMPROVE THE WORLD

By Maria Helena Paulo

I am about to share with you how the worst pain I have ever experienced transformed me into a new and better version of me.

I lost my dad in January 2020 after having lost three of my younger brothers over the previous eight years. It is so painful to lose family and, at the time, I lost focus on everything. I stopped going out with my best friends, which I love to do. I was mentally blocked. I didn't know what to do. I wasn't sleeping enough, not eating, not talking. I had no direction, and I was frustrated.

Being the firstborn daughter, I had to care about my mom and the rest of my family, but I had no energy. Then, one day, I went to Mom's house, and we talked; I found that she was so strong and the only one who didn't need my support. She is so much stronger than me, and I dedicate this chapter to my mom, Luisa.

After around three months of losing Dad, I decided to turn my life around, to renew my life. I started rereading books on personal development and happened to read an article by Sashin Govender, a young millionaire student from Durban,

South Africa. He recommended that I read a book by one of his best coache
Matt Morris.

I am retired from the banking industry, and since August 2018, I hav
been doing part-time network marketing to help out my mom financially. In th
three months since losing my dad, I had lost almost two-thirds of my earning
and a big part of my team because I was not there to work with them. I had lo
all my motivation to do anything, and my level of leadership and authority ha
deteriorated.

So, by reading various articles, I finally found a book subtitled somethin
like: "I was able to finally learn the secrets of stepping up to a powerful position o
authority, and my income skyrocketed!" It was by Matt Morris, who promised t
teach me "exactly what those secrets are that almost nobody knows about. On
It's in your hands; this book can take any entrepreneur from beginner to celebri
status practically overnight."

From that moment, it was as though something clicked inside me, i
my heart and in my mind. I thought I was dreaming, that it couldn't be rea
I even wondered if I was having a vision! So, I decided to purchase the boo
that promised seven secrets to a seven-figure income, but something went wron
during the buying process.

Then, on 7th May, 2020, I received a message from Matt Morris that saic
"Maria Paulo, what happened? I noticed that you tried to purchase my book a fe
hours ago, but, unfortunately, it looks like your order didn't go through. I wante
to check-in and make sure all your questions are answered."

I thought, my God! How can this be real—a celebrity writing to me!? So,
decided to finish the payment process and purchased the e-book. I downloaded,
read, and I watched the videos and the MLM Masterclass audios.

On 8th May, I saw that there was an invitation in my online mailbox
become a co-author to improve the chances of publishing success. I duly filled i
the application form but was not expecting a positive answer, as I was depresse
and had no experience in writing.

I had never written a book, but I remember having a strong vision of doir
something big for my mom, because if she'd' decided to get pregnant durir
difficult times in 1956, then I was not going to let her down by failing to answ

...e call of a millionaire, who was willing to teach me how to win big, just by ...aking a decision. That's another reason for being grateful to my mom, Luisa. ...reams really can come true: I remember being alone in my room when I opened ...y mail on the 14th of May and listening to Matt in his video saying, "Hi, Maria, ...ongrats for being selected as part of the team of co-authors."

Again, I did not believe that he was actually talking to me!

Moms produce many successful people, people who are leading the world, ...illionaires who are positively impacting the lives of other moms and their ...hildren. These people are scientists, entrepreneurs, constructors, and healthcare ...orkers. And they do this by merely deciding to be moms, by transforming that ...ecision into action. They've found the "how-to" of it, they are committed to ...heir decision, and they care for their children. They are motivated, they believe ...n themselves, and they use their power positively.

Finally, I say that the world should thank all moms because, by their ...ecisions and commitment, they can change peoples' lives for the better, so that ...here are smiling faces all over.

Now, let me share with you how far moms can continue doing big things.

Moms, you know how your children are always watching what you do as ...n example. As you want the best life for them, you should make sure that they ...e you doing BIG things.

They don't do what you say, but what you do!

Moms sometimes have to struggle to empower their children, but I say, ..."Woman, go and have freedom of lifestyle; you're powerful, you do have a better ...ay, so go and show the world!"

Moms should encourage other women to do network marketing, as it's ...perfect fit for stay-at-home moms. So, if you're a mom who can imagine and ...elieve that it's possible to become a millionaire, you can bestow freedom and ...elp people.

It's a fact that many women are in business but are not making enough ...oney. One way to start making money is through network marketing, where ...ou make a small initial investment on joining.

In the network marketing industry, there's no age limit, no gender, race, or ...ligious bar, and you don't need a formal education, certificates, or degrees. What you do need is to have a vision, to set up your goals, and surround yourself with positive and successful people.

Moms, what is required is to focus on following the system, on doing what your mentors do, constantly and persistently.

There's only one question you need to ask your customers: Do you want to have extra money? If they say yes, then you close the deal with them, and you earn your commissions by spreading your company worldwide.

Moms, you also need to commit to daily habits, like more time, more freedom, and a lot of money.

Moms, you can and should raise your children, and by doing it, you can transform people, helping them toward better health, wealth, and relationships.

When you feel tired or depressed, you can turn that around and fuel yourself with personal development through seminars, webinars, and reading books.

What I've learned is that we should dream big, think big, and realize that to meet our goals and achieve our dreams, we first have to master our skills. To get the big results you want, you have to put in a lot of hard work.

Another lesson to keep in mind is the old rule of 80/20: only twenty percent of people are seriously working; the other forty percent do nothing; the remaining forty percent do a little. In my experience, it's advisable to foster the discipline of always learning something new to get good results. So, Moms, where do you position yourself within the old 80/20 rule? I have chosen to be part of the twenty percent.

Moms, you should schedule time for exercise because it's good for your health. It may be tough at times, but if you set yourself achievable goals, you will be able to push through, and you'll find it's well worth it. To positively impact the world, you must first improve your self-esteem, be kind to yourself. You don't have to be perfect, but just be the best version of you that you can be. Forgive yourself for your mistakes and protect your mental health. Don't let yourself get lost in a maze of anxiety and fear about things, like the coronavirus, where you don't have all the facts—don't listen to rumor or fake news—get out there and get the facts by listening to the health experts. Then you will be able to forge the best path ahead.

Successful moms start by creating a daily schedule for outdoor time, academic time, home cheers, free time, bedtime, and so on. Moms can create more freedom for their sons and daughters and inspire them through network marketing. Moms have transitioned from working in traditional jobs to building businesses that provide a high-quality lifestyle for their families.

These moms manage their time so that they can be as productive as possible when working from home. They create agreements with kids and spouses that make it much easier for them to grow a business, while still having quality family time. So, again, moms can impact their kids in positive ways, as they build their business by supporting and inspiring them.

I am so grateful for this realization. There are so many moms involved in business, whether working corporate jobs or stay-at-home jobs. Here are some of the solutions to the challenges they face: negotiating agreements with kids, partners, and spouses, traveling together, watching videos together about success stories, or involving your significant ones.

It's critical that your kids see the work that you are doing and the positive results it produces.

Reasons for moms to choose network marketing careers:

1. Moms are looking for flexible hours; you can do network marketing online, via phone, in person, during evenings.

2. Women are usually big supporters of other women and are big on motivating them to succeed, but, in a corporate environment, they often experience fear, criticism, or envy. In contrast, network marketing fosters an atmosphere of love, encouragement, affirmation, and supportive coaching.

3. Spending time around other successful women is exciting and inspiring. After spending time with kids, it's great to have a little bit of time with other moms, but let it be with moms who are both inspired and inspiring and love to have fun while making money.

4. Moms are experts in getting the best value for their money, and network marketing startup costs are generally low. Plus, from your very first sale,

you're already making money.

5. There are no barriers to entry in network marketing, and with mom bringing their experience and know-how from all walks of life, it's th perfect place for them to cultivate faith, improve their level of educatio and work experience.

6. Moms in network marketing enjoy personal transformation, but als build trust networks, get lots of on the job business training, as we as benefiting from attending workshops and webinars. I guarantee tha within two years in the network marketing industry, you will underg a personal transformation that will be worth far more than the extr money you gain. The material things you'll gain are not as valuable as th personal growth and sense of fulfillment you'll experience. It's not wha you get, but who you become—the best version of yourself.

7. Moms like to lead lives of financial independence where they feel they'r making a contribution.

So, you can see that network marketing simply ticks all the boxes for mom looking to improve their own lives and those of their children and families. It's a open, flexible business model that promises rich personal and financial rewards. you want to learn more, I recommend reading Lauren Kinghorn's book, *7 Rockin Reasons Moms Chose Network Marketing Careers*. All mothers, with their work an personal investment in their children, whether they are in paid employment c not, make a vital contribution to the economy of their country. They represent huge and important part of a nation's workforce and productivity and are vital the economy's health.

Therefore, increasing opportunities for working mothers would boost th economy. Coronavirus has impacted the economy, especially for moms workin from home, who are stressed about not being able to engage effectively at wor Clearly, this will cost the economy billions of dollars.

With COVID-19, there are pros and cons to stay-at-home parenting.

ros:

   i.   Increase in child's school performance

  ii.   The child has less stress and aggression

 iii.   Social approval

ons:

   i.   Desire to return to work

  ii.   Higher levels of stress

 iii.   Social isolation for mothers

would like to conclude this chapter by encouraging all moms to stay caring and 'ork on themselves, their children, and families for the benefit of the world.

Today, we know a lot more about the great things that great women ave done and continue to do; they're businesswomen, family carers, students, rofessionals, domestic goddesses—and moms!

While we often recognize the significant contributions that women make to ociety as successful doctors, politicians, and lawyers, as well as in all professional 'alks of life, their overall contribution to a well-balanced and civilized society trough motherhood and caring for others is often overlooked,

To close, I can say all that cleaning work that mostly women end up doing, essential work because without good cleaning and sanitation everybody gets ck!

There is a light inside each one of us that must be nourished, that needs to e cared for to shine brightly, but sometimes it is overlooked, it has not spoken, has not loved.

Give it the music it needs to dance; that light is you, it's within you, but metimes it gets forgotten, yet it's the thing that others most want to see, so let shine.

If you shine, then you give others permission to do the same. So, always imb up and clean the light itself. Always take care of the light within. Don't hide e light. The world needs you to shine.

BIOGRAPHY

Maria Helena Paulo is 63 years old. She was born in Xai Xai, a small village i
Mozambique. She has a Master's degree in economics and has had careers in th
civil service for eighteen years and the banking industry for fifteen years. She love
teaching and has spent fifteen years teaching economics and finance part-tim
at her local university. She retired from the Central bank in 2011 but continue
to serve the banking industry as an executive board member. Two years ago, sh
joined the Worldventures company to travel with family and friends. She love
music, dancing, and helping people. She loves her mom, Luisa, and is married t
Candido; they have two daughters—Sonia and Sheila, and are grandparents t
two lively boys—Caio and Kizua.

Contact Information
Facebook: https://www.facebook.com/mariahelena.paulo.1232

CHAPTER 20

THE KEY FOR LIMITLESS SUCCESS

By Mike Howren

I t was November of 2012 when I received a phone call from an old friend. I can't recall what she said, exactly, but I knew that she was more excited than I'd ever seen her. I do remember that she told me she had something I had to see.

Once she arrived, she pulled up a website on my computer, started playing a video, and I was rolling my eyes within 30 seconds. "Are you pitching me a pyramid scheme right now?" I asked. "I've seen dozens of these companies and presentations, and they don't work. They're a scam and a waste of money. Only the people who join in the beginning make money."

You have probably said the same thing at some point in your life, or maybe you know someone who shared a similar story. I had no exposure to the network marketing industry at the time. Growing up, I was told the key to success was to go to school, get good grades, and find a safe and secure job. So, I went to Kent State University, got my degree in business administration, and entered corporate America. I started working with a marketing company and worked my way up through the ranks over the years. By my mid-twenties, I had become my company's vice-president of sales. There I was with a great job, a great title, and a

six-figure income. "Man, I've made it!" I thought, but as the years went by, I too
on more responsibilities, which meant more time at the office, more stress, an
less time to do the things I wanted to do with the people about whom I cared.

We all know people like that—they make good money, but they have n
time because they are always working. We also know people who have a lot o
time on their hands, but they're broke. I've always been interested in learning ho
I could have both time and money. I was at a point in my life where every decisio
I made came down to two things: could I afford it, and do I have the time to d
it? Despite my good job, I was still living paycheck-to-paycheck, was stressed ou
and time-broke. I needed a change.

So, back to that day in November. I finished watching the networ
marketing presentation. Honestly, I only watched it to be polite to my friend, an
I had every intention of telling her no. In fact, six months prior, I had actuall
seen a presentation from the same company and had said no at the time. Well, th
time, I was introduced to a very successful guy who became a huge mentor in m
life. A mentor—imagine that. I had never even considered seeking out a mento
before. I was too focused on just getting through the week, paying my bills, an
waiting for the weekend. That day, he asked me a question that completely altere
my path in life: "Mike, how many wealthy employees have you ever met?" h
asked.

Now, at the time, I thought that being wealthy just meant having a lot o
money, so I responded rather quickly. "Doctors," I said.

He looked at me and said, "Doctors are broke."

I was confused, and I politely asked, "What in the hell are you talkin
about? Doctors make great money," I said.

"Don't get me wrong," he said, "They might make great money, but they'r
time-broke. If they don't show up at the hospital, they don't get paid. The perso
who has true wealth is the person who owns the hospital. He makes mone
whether he lifts his head off his pillow or not." He then proceeded to teach m
two laws of wealth that have changed my life forever:

Wealth Law #1: You need to have multiple streams of income—not multipl
jobs but multiple streams. Today's average millionaire has seven.

Wealth Law #2: If you don't find a way to make money while you sleep, ou will have to keep working for your money, and you'll end up working until ou die.

This was drastically different advice than I'd received growing up. Getting a ollege education and a good job was all that I'd heard about.

Two things dawned on me that day: one—as long as I was trading time for oney, I could never have both; and two—the teachers from whom I'd learned in hool didn't have their own financial freedom. How could they teach me about nancial freedom if they didn't have it themselves? That day, I made a decision to ay attention to that guy because he had the life I wanted, and that has made all e difference in the world.

I started my network marketing career that day with high hopes and pirations. I was going to "get rich quick." I learned the presentation and began aring that vision with my friends and family. Some joined me, but many did ot, and my excitement began to fade. The negative tapes started to play over d over again in my head, saying, "You're not cut out for this. You're not the pe of person who can have success with this. You have a great job, just focus on at. This is for people who can't find a good job." Months passed, and I was very ustrated and on the verge of giving up. It was then that I had a conversation ith my mentor, and he convinced me to go to the company's next major training ent. I bought a ticket but reluctantly so. I missed a great friend's wedding, but I ew that I had to figure this out if my life was ever going to change.

That weekend, I saw what the industry was all about, and I fell in love. That eekend, I realized something I saw Grant Cardone post on social media years ter:

veryone should be involved in network marketing.

1. For the personal development
2. For the product
3. For the money

p until that point, I had the order reversed. I was trying to make a bunch of oney, but I wasn't working on myself. I had no clue what personal development

was. The last book I'd read was in college. If you don't know, Grant Cardone h
built a $1.4 billion empire in real estate, was named the number one market
to watch by *Forbes Magazine,* and is the founder of the 10X Growth Conferenc
the world's largest business and entrepreneurial conference. He might have just
little more business credibility than your Uncle Buck, who tells you that netwo
marketing is a scam.

I learned something at that event that changed my entire philosophy in lif
your income will always follow your level of personal development; up or dow
it will follow. Have you ever heard of someone winning millions in the lotter
only to find themselves broke a few short years later? They did not learn how
become the type of person necessary to earn that kind of money, and it left the
almost as quickly as it had arrived. Have you ever seen a millionaire lose all
his money only to become a millionaire again a few short years later? This is du
to the self-image these individuals have. A person who is broke views himself
broke, and no matter how much money may fall into his hands, he will spen
it until he returns to where his true self-image lies—that of a broke person. O
the other hand, a rich person views himself as rich, so no matter what losses
experiences, he will do everything possible to get back to his true self-image—th
of a rich person.

We function the same way as a thermostat in our homes. We all ha
financial thermostats programmed for us, and we aren't even aware of it. O
thermostats are programmed from years of us believing certain things abo
ourselves. What you believe about yourself is a byproduct of your environmen
the people around whom you spend the most time, and the programming of yo
brain by you and those around you over the course of your life. I wasn't traine
on this, not in my entire career in corporate America. Instead, I had to learn th
skills necessary for completing my job, knowing that I would be fired if I didr
do my job correctly. My company couldn't care less how I felt about myself—the
wanted only one thing: performance.

In the world of personal development in network marketing, my self-ima
changed. I surrounded myself with people who built me up instead of tearir
me down. I read books on personal development and was surprised to find the
interesting. These books were drastically different than those I'd read in school.

Network marketing and the personal growth I have experienced has changed every aspect of my life. I've made life-long friends, have created countless memories and had invaluable experiences, have traveled the world, and lived life on my own terms. I've been introduced to a group of peers who have pushed me and made me better. I've had mentorship from some of the most successful people I've ever met. I've become a better leader, performer, communicator, partner, friend, son, brother, servant, and an overall better person. Because of this industry, I've learned how to be a business owner, and I have built a multi-million dollar business outside of my network marketing business. I've expanded my mindset and vision and have created and achieved goals that I previously thought impossible.

So, the next time you get a call from a friend or an old acquaintance who has something he wants to share with you, know this: he is not trying to sell you anything. Instead, he has experienced something that has changed his life, and he thought enough of you to pick up the phone to call you. Answer the call and hear him out. You never know if that one phone call might forever change the direction of your life.

Limitless success is never-ending, and it is available to anyone who wishes to unlock it. The key, however, lies within your mind, and the best way for an average person to access that key is to plug into the system of personal development offered through network marketing.

BIOGRAPHY

Mike Howren is a Northeast Ohio native, traditional business owner, six-figure network marketing professional, and an author. Having grown up in the rust belt, Mike learned the importance of a strong work ethic. It is this work ethic and discipline that has carried him through the ranks of corporate America, but it wasn't until he started working harder on himself than he did on his career that he started to see a change in his lifestyle. His passions include traveling with his fiancée, Lindsay, and spending time with his family, golfing, and boating. His current mission in life is to teach others and inspire them to live life on their own terms.

Contact Information
Facebook: https://www.facebook.com/mike.howren
Instagram: https://www.instagram.com/mikehowren/
Website: http://www.michaelhowren.com

CHAPTER 21

LIVING THE DREAM

By Richard Denning

E veryone dreams, it's the way God made us. We dream about the future, we dream about how things are going to turn out, the great job we are going to have, the vacations, the big house, great family, and plenty of money. We dream about the things we are going to accomplish, how we are going to change the world and make a difference. All those things can come true if you have the right mindset. If you are willing to do today what others aren't, you will have tomorrow what others can't.

Everyone has their own idea of what it means to "Live the Dream." For some, it means financial freedom or the freedom of more quality time. For others, it's owning their own business, being their own boss, or working at something that they feel passionate about. God has given me a passion for helping other people. That's why I have written this book—to help you to discover what "Living the Dream" means for you. I hope that, after you've read it, a whole new world opens up for you and that you will learn how to dream again.

Before we get into the good stuff, let me tell you a little bit about myself. My name is Richard Denning. My wife is Timberly. We have two children and two grandchildren. I live in northern middle Tennessee, about one hour north of Nashville, Tennessee, in the Fairfield community. I have lived here all my life. I am a fulltime farmer and, over the years, I have raised, cattle, hogs, pheasants, quail, chukar, bird dogs, rabbits, corn, soybeans, wheat, oats, barley, sunflower milo, tobacco, and, in 2019, I started growing hemp for CBD oil. I also own hunting preserve and a ten-acre pay lake. Diversification is key to being successfu on the farm. If one or two of the commodities are down, some are steady, an some, hopefully, are up. Farming is a great life, but it takes a lot of hard work– precise planning, guts, nerves, and prayers that Mother Nature will be kind to t throughout the year. Farming is probably the biggest gamble in life. We roll th dice every year. It has been said, "Give a farmer a dollar and he will spend ten Farmers are probably the most optimistic people in the world.

My entrepreneurship began as a young boy when I started raising rabbits t sell. I would also ride my three-speed bike around the area and pick up discarde coke bottles, then take them to the store and get five cents per bottle, which wa pretty good money for a young boy. I bought a lot of Super Bubble, chewin gum, cokes, and peanuts. Some of you know what I mean. I also worked at th high school basketball games for my dad, where I started collecting silver coin I would trade my money for the coins and one-half dollars. My dad taught hig school agriculture for over thirty years, and my mom taught elementary schoo for more than forty years. As I grew up on the farm, I learned hard work an commitment from both Mom and Dad. But life on the farm was not all work– there was play, too. For instance, Dad built a baseball field where we practice Little League and Babe Ruth baseball and then played church league softball fo several years. We hunted, we fished, and attended church every Sunday. To u that was "Living the Dream."

I played football, basketball, and baseball all through junior high and hig school. I graduated valedictorian. I had big dreams. I had to decide to either go t college or stay on the farm. I decided to stay on the farm. I had lived the drea all through school. Now one chapter of my life was ending, and a new one wa beginning. I got married, my wife was going to college, and, for the first time, had bills to pay, real bills. I wasn't afraid of hard work. I was young, healthy, an full of energy; I was ready to take on the world.

Farming is a rollercoaster ride. Like any profession, it has its ups an downs. I thought that I was "Living the Dream," but there were times when I ha to question that assumption. Sure, I was my own boss, owned my own busines

nd I could take off anytime I wanted. Except that I didn't; I hadn't had a vacation
n years. Wow! I realized that my business owned me, and I didn't even know
. I loved what I was doing, but I was getting older, and farming was getting
arder. It wasn't as much fun as it used to be. The decisions were getting more
omplicated—payroll, insurance, and on and on. I had to continue to increase my
arming operation to survive. It seemed never ending, and it was becoming more
emanding, while profits were getting smaller.

But I was always looking for more income through new ideas. So, when my
iend invited me to take a look at an idea that she was excited about, I thought
was too busy. I'd seen those things before. They don't work, and I didn't want
o sell products. I almost didn't go along to find out more, but I am so glad
at I did because I was pleasantly surprised. I saw a way to save a lot of money
nd create a really good residual income with the help of a team. I knew about
amwork. I had been on many teams during my lifetime, and I knew that a team
ould accomplish more than one individual. The residual income really got my
tention. I saw a way to cut back on my farming operation and supplement my
tirement. Now my dreams were beginning to change. The idea of "Living the
ream" began to take on a whole new meaning.

Warren Buffet says, "If you don't find a way to make money while you
eep, you will work until you die."

Do you want to work until you die? Do you want to do what you are doing
ow for the rest of your life? What's going to change in the next year, the next
ve years, ten years, or twenty years? Are you dreaming? Sometimes your dreams
ange. In my case, my first dream was to be debt-free and have enough money
o buy anything I wanted. I accomplished that. But I had to put in sixty, seventy,
ghty hours a week to have that lifestyle. Because of that, I missed so much time
ith my kids growing up. I was time broke. I had created a monster that I couldn't
t away from. Farming was taking all my time. I had been taught to work hard,
o your best, and you will make it. That's what we are taught in school. That's
hat society teaches us, the forty, forty, forty plan: Work forty hours a week, for
rty years, and retire on forty percent of the income you were making. But that's
ot enough to live on. Besides, during those forty years, you are helping build
omeone else's DREAM! Why not start building your own DREAM?

I am writing this during the COVID-19 pandemic. Many people have been laid off or lost their jobs. A second stream of income would have made much easier for them to deal with the situation. Money is not everything, but sure does take the rough edges off.

"Dreams don't work unless you do!"

Most of us start with big dreams, then life happens. We go to work, help build someone else's dream, come home, eat, and go to bed. We get stuck in an endless, repeating cycle. Over time, our dreams begin to fade away and get crushed by life. Then there are the others who tell us that we're crazy for having dream, saying, "You can't do that!" They don't dream, and they don't want you to dream either. NOTE: DON'T LISTEN TO THEM! They don't pay your bill. A wise man once said, "Sometimes the things we regret most in life are the risk that we never took."

What does "Living the Dream" mean? Is it possible? I believe that network marketing is the vehicle to accomplishing your dreams.

When I was first introduced to network marketing, I was working sixty to eighty hours a week. I had no time to spare. But, you know, we make time for what we want to do, and for what is important. I looked at several network marketing opportunities, but none of them seemed to be the right fit. I didn't really want to sell products. So, when my friend asked us to look at something that she was excited about, my wife and I were a little reluctant. But along we went, and we were really surprised at what we found. This time, it seemed to be the right fit and the right timing for us. NOTE: Find something that you love doing, and you won't work another day in your life.

Here's what happened to me: I had "Lived the Dream," but it had faded away until I was no longer dreaming, but I didn't even notice; I was consumed with farming. I was caught up in the rat race of life. Realizing this, I was open to looking at a new opportunity, and what I saw was a way to change my life for the better. This network marketing idea was exciting, and I began to dream again. For the first time in years, I was excited. I saw and talked to regular people who had transformed their lives from a mundane lifestyle to an exciting adventure. I knew that that was what I wanted.

It started with a thought; "If they can do it, I can do it." The wheels in my mind began to spin, and I couldn't sleep for a week. Everything starts in the mind, with belief. If you can see it and you believe it, you can achieve it. The mind is a powerful thing: You become what you think about. I began to think positively. I learned about personal growth, which I had never heard of before. I started reading books like *Think and Grow Rich*, *The Magic of Thinking Big*, and *Rich Dad Poor Dad*. I started watching videos of successful people. Personal growth has helped me in every area of life. I was so excited that I was going to sign up everyone I knew. Surely, they would be as excited as I was? But that wasn't how it happened, and I started to get knocked down. How many times do you keep getting back up? One more time? I love the great outdoors and like to deer hunt. I learned it from sitting patiently in the tree stand in the darkest hour just before dawn. The Bible talks about a time for everything, but it doesn't mention anything about a time to quit. Don't quit! Take it from one of the greatest basketball players of all time: "I missed more than 9000 shots in my career. I've lost almost 300 games. Twenty-six times I've been trusted to take the game-winning shot and missed. I've failed over and over again in my life. And that is why I succeeded."—Michael Jordan.

With the help of others, you can get back up. You can succeed. Don't quit until the miracle happens.

FINAL THOUGHTS

There's never a wrong time to start dreaming. Go for it!

Be open to new ideas. There's one that is right for you!

Nothing happens until someone gets excited. Be Excited! Be all in!

Do you want to change your life and your family's life for the better? Do you want to leave a positive legacy that will last for years after you are gone? If you do, you will have to take some risks. Remember, I mentioned earlier, "Often, the things that we regret most in life are the risks we were never willing to take."

Let me leave you with this thought:

Life is short, so don't let the sun go down on you before you "LIVE YOU DREAM."

To God, Be the Glory, for with Him, all things are possible.

BIOGRAPHY

Richard Denning was born and raised on a farm in middle Tennessee, the hom of country music, and has over forty years of farming experience. He loves hunt, fish, play sports, and be in the great outdoors. He became a full-time farm right after high school, helping feed the world. Over the years, he has also create an outstanding hunting business, Meadow Brook Game Farm, where he has m people from all over the world. Creating multiple streams of income has bee instrumental in being a successful farmer. Richard has a passion for helping other In this book, he talks about *Living the Dream* and how his farming experience ha helped him successfully launch his network marketing business and allowed hi the opportunity to show others how to create an extra stream of residual incom

Contact Information
Facebook: https://www.facebook.com/richard.denning.716

CHAPTER 22

THE ULTIMATE SUCCESS FORMULA

By Romacio Fulcher

In "The Ultimate Success Formula," my goal is to provide you with something simple yet profound that will help you in every area of your life, be it spirituality, finances, relationships, health, or your community. I will give you access to a formula that has never failed to work for me, no matter the situation.

I graduated from high school with a 2.5 GPA. I dropped out of college after 1.5 years, so I can tell you firsthand that I'm not the sharpest tool in the shed. In my 42 years on earth, the one thing I can tell you is that I'm really good at keeping things stupidly simple. The world we live in today is so complicated. There is so much going on that it is easy to feel as if you are drowning, lost, or confused. My aim today is to share a simple formula with you that is sure to work in every area of your life. I am excited to impart this to you, but I do ask one thing in return—when you read this, I want you to apply it instantly and be blessed because of it.

Let us talk about my Ultimate Success Formula. The definition of success, according to the dictionary, is the progressive realization of a worthwhile goal or worthy ideal. This means that the key to being successful is always to be sure that you are making progress. The reason why many of us become trapped and entangled in frustration in certain areas of life is that we are just not making

progress. This is why I am confident my formula will change everything for yo
It is truly a game-changer.

Are you ready?
Let us begin.

The first thing about the success formula is that it is critically important that yo
know your ultimate outcome. Consider your health, for example. If your go
is to lose weight, you must be clear as to exactly how much weight you want t
lose—this is your outcome. Your outcome must be crystal clear. It cannot b
blurry. Clarity is power.

If your goal is to make money, you must be specific as to exactly ho
much money you would like to make—this is your outcome. Your target mu
be precise.

If your goal is to find a mate, you must decide upon your preference
Consider the personality traits of the person you would feel comfortable datin
or marrying—this is your outcome. This is important because if you don't kno
your outcome, you may be tempted to settle for anyone. Remember—clarity
power; you must know your outcome to be successful. There are no exceptio
to this rule.

Whether your goal is about family, relationships, or money, you have t
know your outcome, and specifically what you want.

The second thing is to take massive steps towards achieving your outcom
This is the fun part. Notice how I did not say to take baby steps—I meant t
take massive steps. If your outcome is to go from earning $20,000 to $100,000
year in income, you must initiate a massive amount of action towards achievin
your goal, according to my formula. This is important—you must take massiv
action. The more action you take towards achieving your goal, the sooner you wi
achieve the goal. This is critically important for you to understand. When yo
take massive action, you reach your goal much faster because you put more energ
and effort into it. This applies to everything.

I took massive action when dating as a young man. You can probab
imagine what that means. You will never be ashamed if you take massive actio
instead of taking just a little bit of action. Not only does this formula work

very area in your life, but it works every single time. All you need is the courage to take massive action towards achieving what you want. If you want something to happen right away, you have to be courageous and take massive action.

Number three is to always have a coach. What this means is that when you have a goal in mind, you should find someone who has already accomplished that goal. Let me explain why having a coach is important. Every single one of us has said, "I wish I had known then what I know now," at least once in our lives. You have probably also heard that hindsight is 20/20. With experience comes wisdom. Wisdom comes from banging your head against the wall as you make mistake after mistake until you eventually figure the problem out and become wiser. It also comes from learning from someone else's mistakes. This means that when you are trying to accomplish any goal, it is always wiser for you to learn how to achieve it from a coach who has already accomplished what you are trying to do.

I have a coach in every area of my life. Be it spiritual, health, money-making, or saving and investing, I have a mentor no matter what I do in life because time the only thing in life that you cannot get back. You can make money and lose money, you can lose weight and gain weight, but the one thing you can't get back time, so you must value your time, and to do that, it is smarter and wiser if you always have a coach.

Consider business, for a second, and the goal of making more money for what you're doing. Find a good coach. This does not ring true only for business. It can be for any area in life including spirituality, relationships, and health. To find good coach, go online and look up the type of coach for which you are looking. Make a note of the top ten or 20 in the field, and find out who they are—this is secret number one. Secret number two is to find out how to get in contact with prospective coaches. When you do, ask them a single question: what do I have to to make it worth your while to coach me on what I want to know? These two simple steps are how you can attract any kind of coach you want.

The question from secret number two is powerful because when you find the coach, you're not asking him/her to give you something for nothing. You are telling the coach that you are willing to work for what they know, exchanging your work for his/her knowledge. It shows the coach that you don't want something for nothing, which is very attractive to a coach and says a lot about you. Once again, it's really simple to find a coach. Look them up online—the top 10 or 20 that profession. Number two, get a hold of them and ask them what it is that yo would have to do to make it worth their while for them to teach you what the know. This is step number three. Always, always, always have a coach.

Finally, step number four of the ultimate success formula: gauge you approach. Let's say you have the first three right—if step number four is n working, then change your approach. You need to have an acute sense to kno if your actions are bringing you closer to what you want, and if things are n working for you.

Now that you have the four steps of the Ultimate Success formula, I wa to share all of the areas of my life in which I use this formula to be successful. Th is the most important formula of my entire life, so let us take a look.

In the area of health and fitness, I have used this formula, knowing m outcome. For example, right now, I am in the process of losing 23 pounds in 3 days. I am 223 pounds right now, and I want to be 200 pounds within 30 days— know my outcome.

Step 2: I'm taking massive action toward my goal. What does that mean? As a example, I prepare the meals that I eat every day. I work out with a trainer usir a specific type of workout that will help me to reach my goal.

Step three is critical: I have a coach. As an example, I am learning from someor who has already lost 25 pounds in 30 days, and I am doing exactly what he did. am eating the same foods and doing the same workouts.

Finally, step four—let us just say if I am 25 days into the program and I am eatir right, and I am working out, but I am not making any progress towards n goal of losing 23 pounds in 30 days. That is when I would change my approac according to step four.

I use this formula in every area of my life.

Let us talk about making money.

Years ago, in December of 2016, I was actually broke. I had made son very poor choices with my money and found myself in a position where I w roke. I believe that if something is broken, you should fix it, and I used the formula once again.

I knew my outcome: to save $1,000,000 over 12 months—not make 1,000,000 but save $1,000,000 over 12 months.

tep one: I knew my outcome.

tep two: I took massive action. I got involved with a business, and I went to work ke you would not believe. I worked harder in that business in the first 30 days an I have ever worked in my life.

tep three: I made sure I had a coach, someone who has already achieved this goal efore, and I made sure I did exactly what they told me to do.

tep four: if I had not seen progress by following the formula, I would have anged my approach. I continually gauged my results to see if I was getting oser to my outcome. Guess what? It worked!

n December 1, 2016, I was broke, and by December 7, of 2017, not only had I ade millions of dollars, but I had saved over $1,000,000 liquid in my personal ank account for the very first time in my life, and I did it over 12 months. I made pies of it, had it framed, and posted it all over my house. My point is that it orks in every area of life.

Let me end by asking you this: how many chances do you give a newborn aby to walk? The answer is: as many times as it takes. Some babies walk in n months, and some of them walk much later in life, but by the time that aby is seven-years-old, all babies walk. This is why I say to gauge your results. If mething is not working, change your approach and gauge your results. If it is ill not working, change your approach again and gauge your results. If it is still ot working, change your approach and gauge your results. These four steps will ork in every area of your life. They are very simple—extremely simple! Do it ow, and I promise you that your life will instantly improve.

I'm Romacio Fulcher, The California Kid.

BIOGRAPHY

Romacio Fulcher is a well-respected international leader, trainer, coach, and much sought-after mentor. He is a highly successful entrepreneur. He tried the traditional college path and quickly found that it wasn't for him. Instead, he began as a cold caller, getting leads for a mortgage company. Under the owner's mentorship he mastered the business, ultimately going on to start his own mortgage and real estate company to become a self-made millionaire by the age of 25. He was introduced to his MLM mentor and the industry of network marketing about ten years ago. He applied what he learned once again to become a top leader and earner. Although Romacio has earned millions of dollars, his heart is in training and inspiring others to transform their lives by helping others earn supplemental income along the way.

Contact Information
Facebook: https://www.facebook.com/romacio.fulcher
Instagram: https://www.instagram.com/romaciofulcher/
YouTube: https://www.youtube.com/channel/UC1zB-1jmoOpJE_hg_aEPNZC

CHAPTER 23

SHADES OF GREY

By Samantha Jung-Fielding

"For someone so intelligent, what on earth was I thinking? How did it get to this?" These thoughts tumbled around my mind as I gingerly touched my scalp, feeling the coin-sized bald patches where my hair was ripped out.

Something did not add up. Why did I stay in an abusive relationship with man who tried to murder me four times? How much more would it take for me to wake up and smell the coffee? As things turned out, only one single well-aimed punch, not leveled at me this time. Instead, he hit the dog. He struck so hard I heard its skull crack. At that precise moment, I finally understood that unless I acted quickly, one of us would die.

It was January 1996, and I was 28 years old. One week after that incident, I ran away taking only the clothes on my back. I drove out of Belgium and down into France, heading for the ferry back to the UK. At a safe distance, I phoned him. His voice raged down the line, irrational, coercive, and demanding: "Did you take the TV? When I get hold of you, I'm going to rearrange your face. You'd better get yourself home right now and sort this out."

Although I initially felt I had the upper hand, over the next nine months, I desperately wanted to go back every single day. It was impossible to make a simple decision on my own. The psychologist outlined how the abuser and I had become co-dependent.

I was floored. Me? Co-dependent? What do you mean? My mother has dependency issues. Not me! I'm Miss Independent, the most reliable one. I'm the person the family depends on to hide family secrets, and being the eldest child, I was there to always save the day.

Except I didn't save this day. And now, locked in with my abuser, I had to find the key.

So, how did it get to this? What exactly had I been thinking? I was the first person in my family to go to university, yet how useful is intelligence if you still make stupid life decisions?

It was a revelation when I discovered how the mind works. Simply put, it a game of two halves— the conscious and the unconscious! Everybody instantly relates to the conscious mind because its job is to think and reflect, to make logical and rational decisions. In university, my conscious mind was continually stimulated, daily contemplating new ideas. This is why the conscious is also called the thinking mind.

However, did you know the conscious only represents about 10% of the mind's total capacity? The remaining 90% lies in the unconscious, whose main function is storage and processing. The unconscious is responsible for automatic body functions (like your heart beating, digesting food, and correctly positioning your limbs for sitting, walking, or even climbing the stairs). The unconscious carefully files everything you ever learned or experienced, plus it stores your values, beliefs, emotions, coping mechanisms, routines, and habits. The unconscious also known as the feeling mind.

In this marriage of the minds, it's critical to note your unconscious operational from the moment of conception, while your conscious mind first awakens around your 7th birthday.

As a result, during the formative years, small children absorb everything without question. Their surroundings are readily accepted as a baseline of "normal" reference point, and they are heavily influenced by the people around them. In short, without any filters, they act like sponges.

This is all the more alarming when you realize your early patterns set a foundation for the rest of your life. This means your brain was programmed by a toddler, who mostly copied examples handed on by past generations (i.e., your parents, or even older!). Of course, you had no idea things could happen any other way. So, when the controls were passed to you, you left everything in place, permitting those automatic and established patterns to run their natural course.

And the fly in the ointment? Unproductive historical family blueprints. This explains why in January 1996, I was repeating patterns from my mother's personal history. It's unlikely to surprise you that my mum also survived an abusive relationship, including a murder attempt when I was seven years old.

To recap, intelligence (or lack of it) was not a factor in my abuse. Nor did it matter what I had been consciously thinking. Because I was unconsciously following a pattern learned literally at my mother's knee. And, it got to this because I had not yet learned how to break this unproductive cycle.

Shocking! Unfortunately, the implied consequence was even more severe. Unless I acted quickly, I would subject my unborn children to the same fate.

So, where to next? Brazenly attempting to avoid my mother's alcohol dependency, I had already shifted from being independent to co-dependent. Moreover, it's not like she never warned against the pitfalls of extremity. As a child, I repeatedly heard: "You're so black and white. What about some shades of grey?"

Was I to infer grey is the color of inter-dependence? The very definition of black and white (or polar opposites) is that neither exists without its opposite. There cannot be yes without no, day without night, or up without down. Perhaps the crux of extremity is inter-dependence, and any spotlight must shine on the continuum between?

Unfortunately, I was stuck in extremity. Looking back, I noticed I was always out on a limb. Mum named my brothers in honor of their uncles. Yet, I was called Samantha—after the witch on television. In 1964, Elizabeth Montgomery took the lead role in Bewitched. A twitch of her nose launched a fashion for naming daughters, which reached me in 1967. Years later, I discovered the origin of my name is Aramaic, and it means "the listener."

I grew up believing I was magical with the unshakeable conviction I was put on this earth for remarkable feats. My formative years provided few examples,

Aristotle's wisdom set my course: "We are what we repeatedly do. Excellence, then, is not an act, but a habit."

According to Dictionary.com, "A habit is an acquired behavior pattern regularly followed until it has become almost involuntary." John Dryden said, "We first make our habits, and then our habits make us." Experience had already shown me that habits run the show, but I was also painfully aware of what goes on behind the scenes. Emotions (especially negative ones) muddy the waters.

My mum demonstrated how those with unresolved negative emotion (like anger, sadness, fear, hurt, or guilt) tend towards the systematic repetition of problematic behavior. Consider the use of stimulants (e.g., cigarettes, alcohol, coffee, sugar, recreational drugs), binge eating, video games, road rage, cyclical abusive relationships, overthinking and procrastination. What mum didn't know was that getting rid of the underlying emotion can be enough to morph behavioral issue into a productive pattern.

Emotional release is an immensely powerful and transforming process which unhooks the negative feelings from past memories. This allows you to remember an event or person without re-experiencing the sensations that were previously associated with it. For years I blamed my mother for ruining my childhood with her drinking. By taking full responsibility for my own future and releasing this extreme perspective of my past, I chose to feel compassion for Mum. In doing so, I paved the way for a positive connection with my own daughter.

In his book "The Power of Habit," Charles Duhigg highlights how every habit is unconsciously designed to produce an emotional reward. Realistically speaking, any effective and long-term behavior change must, therefore, begin with emotional release.

Unpicking enough formative patterns creates a wide, open space to accommodate your most eagerly anticipated emotional reward. When I abruptly quit my second marriage, nobody understood my choice. However, I was aware my carefully crafted happiness was lopsided, and I was gifted a moment of clarity. Propping it up further was establishing yet another dysfunctional dependency.

I have long cherished the idea of two equal and opposite people coming together to develop a wonderful continuum (or legacy) of well-rounded children. Over the years, I was gifted with three magnificent boys. I always dreamed of aving a daughter, but becoming a single parent at 41 shattered this lingering ope.

Since marrying my third husband, I repeatedly joke that on good days we e equal, but on bad days we are very opposite. However, it was no joke when fell pregnant just two weeks into our relationship. True to form, Mum was less an encouraging when I announced the news: "Oh God! Not another one!"

In authentic witch tradition, my daughter showed up 13 days late. Having ready waited 19 years for this child, a few more nights of sleep were neither here or there. Her entrance into this world was bold and breath-taking. She birthed nexpectedly at home, with a theatrical fall into the toilet.

I already knew her name would be Maya, after my mother's mother. nagine my surprise when someone later told me Maya means "mother" in the upi language.

A few months before Maya turned 3, our family emigrated from the UK New Zealand. Known to the children as "Yorkshire Nan," my mum was eartbroken. She was sure she would never see me again. Barely a year later, she ad a stroke which left her paralyzed down the left side. Some months after, I flew ack to the UK to surprise her for her 70th birthday. That was the last time she w me. After that, she slowly deteriorated and passed away shortly before Maya rned 7.

While mum waited for her curtain to fall, I rang her daily. She could no nger speak, so the nurse held the receiver to her ear and told me Mum smiled l the way through our calls. I chose to remain in New Zealand for the funeral, d my best friend from childhood attended on my behalf. There is a significant me zone difference, so I had just jumped into the car with Maya when I saw a hone message flash up from my friend containing pictures of my mother's wake.

Apparently, "A Whiter Shade of Pale" was at the top of the charts when I as born, and Mum had requested this song be played at her funeral. Without arning, the first melancholy notes drifted from the car radio as I swiped through e photos on my phone. Unexpectedly, Mum's coffin flashed onto my screen, d I began bawling. From the seat behind, a small arm crept around my neck as y daughter asked: "What is it? Is it your mum? It's OK, mama. Just remember hen you were a little girl with Yorkshire Nan."

Maya's simple words of comfort contained wisdom beyond her year Deepak Chopra says that to break through ancestral bonds that inhibit you ability to create the life you deserve, you have to understand where they originat

No doubt you know someone who has spent a lifetime seeking. Yet, th answer is right there before you. Your family blueprint is already cast in black an white. It's the shades of grey that seek your attention.

I implore you to tread with compassion as you release negative emotior and unpick your formative programming. Your very existence is a formidab gift. Take the opportunity to design your unique pattern of productive cycles an happiness habits.

And be mindful that your children will copy your examples (good an bad!). So, I strongly suggest weaving slings and arrows of outrageous fortur through your shades of grey. Therein lies real magic!

BIOGRAPHY

Samantha Jung-Fielding is an award-winning speaker, author, and performan specialist in the field of habit formation and behavior change. Mast hypnotherapist, master NLP practitioner, and certified business mentc Samantha believes unconscious brain and body patterns hold the ultimate secr to your success. Corporate burnout led Samantha to establish a charity, co-foun a business networking organization, and develop a radio chat show. She al launched diverse businesses, initially in traditional fields before expanding in network marketing to deepen her reach. When her family immigrated to Ne Zealand in 2012, Samantha and her husband opted to raise their children on small alpaca farm in South Auckland. Had they understood the alpaca predilectic for mischief, they might have thought twice about this choice.

Contact Information
Facebook: https://www.facebook.com/samjungf
Instagram: https://www.instagram.com/sam_jungf/
Website: http://www.happinessence.co.nz

CHAPTER 24

THE IMMACULATE JOURNEY OF A FAITHFUL WARRIOR

By Serah W. Muiruri

As I walk on my journey, my view of the world is one comprised of many dots, intrinsically connected and unique in their formation, the world would be incomplete if these dots were not strategically positioned to complete the whole. I am amazed at the purpose of each dot, each of them leading to my final destination; without any of these dots, that destination would not be as intended. Often, the purpose of the dot is not revealed on the surface, and if it is, its significance does not fall into place until the end approaches. As I toy with these thoughts, I realize that life is an entity forever unfolding, one that is full of contrast, complexity, uncertainty, confusion, mystery, and above all, vulnerability. These attributes continuously shape who we are day by day, season by season, and year by year. It is a maze that never ends, from its inception and our grand entrance into the world until the time we take our last breaths at the end of our incredible journeys and onto the next one, a rebirth into that unknown world we get to experience beyond our time here, on earth. We are, for today. When our mission is accomplished, we are gone, a little while later. During it all, the world continues to evolve in ways unimaginable. Our world is quite different from th of our ancestors. What determines our existence? Our core beings? Our essence Is this the philosophical dilemma of nature or nurture? I can't help but think th how we end is shaped by who we are as unique beings, our genetic compositio our upbringing, our cultural backgrounds, our spirituality, our metamorphos based on our individual experiences, and above all, the choices we make along th way. These choices are critical in crafting the masterpiece of our valuable selve When these choices are in-line with our core values, we are more fulfilled, ar consequently, a healthy equilibrium is born.

As I compile these words, my desire is to speak to someone out there wh is struggling on her journey in a world that is often quite unforgiving and l her know that the world can and is still a beautiful place, in spite of the da clouds. No matter what you face at the moment, the sunrise is always visible c the horizon. My mission and ultimate desire is to spread hope to the hopeless, plant a seed of joy in those at their lowest point in life, and to let those in despa know that it is in those desperate moments that a new "us" comes to be. Greatne is derived from atrocities. These critical moments propel us toward somethir more significant, that promises a greater tomorrow. If we allow ourselves to ha that experience, it will prove better than the day before.

Here's an extract from a blog post I wrote on March 12, 2014, titled
"Uncovering Our Hidden Treasures – Our Childhood Dreams."

All of us had childhood dreams. At some point, we all wondered what we were goi to be when we grew up. Then, we woke up one morning to discover that our childho dreams and hidden treasures had been lost along the way. How did we get here fast? Where did the time go? All of us inevitably get caught in the proverbial rat ra speeding through life, entangled in our desire to sustain ourselves. Then, slowly b surely, time creeps away only to discover that our childhood dreams have been forev shattered. Our childhood dreams reflect the joys of yesterday and our hopes for t future. We should all protect these dreams, feed them, and encourage them to grow. must take care of our dreams, for someday they may take care of us.

I believe we are all destined to craft our paths as we nurture our uniq individualities, which only we can define. This uniqueness is what separates us fro hers. Our goal in life should be to walk along this path without losing sight of who e are as individuals. It is critical to adopt a mindset that allows us to live lives of urpose, no matter the situation. We are drawn to be clinicians in the human services eld because we want to give back to society, be it giving time or talent, always guided y the philosophy that we are our brothers' keepers. We are great at serving others, but is easy to get lost doing the very thing we love the most. As my brother's keeper, I allenge everyone to do a little soul searching this season—take a brisk walk, feed the irds, listen to your favorite music, do some gardening, or share a cup of coffee, tea, r a meal with a friend you haven't seen in years. Do whatever appeals to you. Let us visit our childhood dreams to renew them. They say that it is in the giving that we ceive, but to receive, we must learn how to give to ourselves first so we can give more others. We have all been given what we need; it is time to rediscover our purposes in fe, which will ultimately help to shape our destinies.

Let's dig up our hidden treasures and childhood dreams.

log Reflection:

wrote this blog about five years ago upon my CEO's request, which was based on king a reflective journey through my life. At that moment, I realized there were ommon themes in my life that were instrumental in shaping me into who and hat I am today. My being is a product of many things, and most are referenced my abstract. Vulnerability has been a constant in my life as far back as I can member. I joined the Mary Leakey Girls School for my A-levels in 1988 at e age of 17. I was only going to spend two years at the boarding school before hoped to enroll in a local University in Nairobi, Kenya, upon graduation. It as the very first time I would be leaving the nuclear family of my parents and blings. I was young, meek, lonely, shy, and unsure. I was consumed by these elings as a youngster, at it eventually had an impact on my academics. Back in e day, Kenya only had four fully-fledged universities, and only the cream of the op could attend these institutions. I certainly knew I had the brains, but my ruggles hindered my desire to be the best I could. I barely survived, made few iends, and basically became a lost introvert in the large crowd. My only goal was get through those two years, and I would be miraculously fine.

Two years later, I was back in the village, having been left behind whi. my colleagues headed to those higher institutions. How could someone like m someone who was "First Division" material, be in this vulnerable position. I wa 19 before I realized I needed to gather the courage to face the world head-on. . spark of hope was born within me, which was ultimately a defining momen I will be forever grateful to my parents and the rest of my family for believin in me and instilling the value of hope, which would be incredibly useful in m journey of self-discovery. I would soon become a high school teacher—a goo milestone—and that was only the beginning. After a long struggle and man challenges, my parents found a way to send me to the US for further studies. Tha was the turning point in embarking on my journey of discovery.

It was a hot summer's day in August 1992 when I left Kenya for the US It was my first time on a plane, and it was a long flight. I landed in Boston, MA with mixed emotions. As I navigated my way in that foreign land, I realized tha my life was bigger than me, and my experiences at MLGS had not only prepare me for good grades but something bigger. These experiences gave me the too and ammunition I needed to succeed in the US in the absence of family ties, an with only a few friends with the same life experience as me. From that point or I knew I needed to craft my life not only to realize my dreams but to help othe realize theirs as well, my family included. As the firstborn in an African famil it was expected that I would share the responsibility of helping raise my sibling but now that I was in the "land of milk and honey," my responsibilities extende to those in my community.

Expanding Responsibilities

As a Catholic girl who almost joined a convent, the life I have lived has been i line with what I perceive to be my purpose. My faith in God has been instrument in this, and without it, I fully acknowledge that I would not be who I am toda Being the first one in my family to travel abroad—and nearly the first youn woman from my village (in rural Ngarariga, Limuru, Kenya) to leave Kenya further her studies—I became a key player in assisting families with young adul interested in joining me in the US. It was a task I executed willingly, as it is what was destined to do. Yes, I made many sacrifices along the way. Often, I could no e how I could continue, given that I was earning meager wages and attending ollege while assisting others do the same. My parents could not pay for tuition es because it was an impossible undertaking, coupled with the fact that I was erceived to be a responsible adult at that point.

To remain purposeful became my goal, and I focused on it. Today, my ctions have had a positive impact on many families. By allowing myself to be a elfless instrument of giving, dreams were born, and they continue to be fulfilled. Most of all, my siblings were able to add to my pool of successful stories, and I ow have the joy of being a part of their successes, as well as that of the others ho have crossed my path over the years. In doing this, I gained much more than would have, had I focused solely on myself.

Marriage and divorce were important milestones in my life, and perhaps the ery best example of life's complexities and conflicts. Of all of the vulnerabilities have experienced, these are significant reference points for me. I was married in happy ceremony on a lovely fall day on November 13, 1999, to a gentleman I nought was my best friend. We had, after all, been everything to each other for everal years prior to the big day, and everything was just great. As fate would ave it, my marriage crumbled ten years later. To say I was devastated would e an understatement, especially considering the added tragedies associated with ne painful break-up. How could the thing I thought the most natural be that omplicated? As a childless African woman, the thought of being divorced was eyond painful. How did I end up here? How or where did I go wrong? What id I have to show for it? Why me? These and endless other questions rang like nnoying bells in my head, and a daily constant for many years following. My ivorce was downright nasty, and the experience was unbearable, ranging from omestic violence, immigration threats, societal biases, and invasion of privacy, ulminating with video from cameras placed in my dwelling and vehicles. I was ollowed and monitored every step of the way, making fear my sad reality. My oon-to-be-ex accused me of poisoning him when his health suffered a downturn. was a baseless accusation, with no scientific evidence to back it up, a ridiculous legation. The status of his health only served to prolong my agony, as I was orced to halt divorce proceedings until he got better. It was a hurtful, grossly ainful, and trying time.

My world had changed, and now, my community doubted me. My only true confidants were immediate family members and a handful of close friends who numbered no more than three people at that point. I struggled to pick up the pieces, knowing I had no other choice. My faith in God kept me going, magnifying my resilience to greater heights. Amidst all of this, I focused on my job and caregiving responsibilities for "my Jen." Her being in my life gave me a sense of value and a higher purpose, keeping me grounded and focused. My coworkers at the time were a great source of support as well, and I remain forever indebted to all of them. It was at this lowest point in my life that I discovered an appreciation of and beauty in being alone as a journey of self-discovery. For the first time, I was able to distinguish between loneliness and being alone. My inner-strength was amplified; it was, indeed, the time for rebirth. Jen remains my purpose today, as do all of my nieces and nephews, who also give me a sense of validation. Nathan and Nayva have been especially instrumental in my healing process. I now know, for a fact, that my life is still unfolding. My parents, siblings, George, Martin, Grace, and Damaris, as well as my extended family, have continued to believe in me even when my strength appears shaken. I know my well-being matters to them, and particularly to my parents, who are aging gracefully.

Letting go of the bitterness was another facet allowing me to enjoy life after divorce as it was meant to be. It was not a simple decision; it was, however, necessary for me to move forward. Trusting that this milestone was part of my ongoing journey, I accepted the situation as it was. Thus far, I have gone through restoration period, and by God's Grace, my success story is still unfolding. I know all too well that in faith, my destiny is well-crafted and spectacularly designed.

As a life coach, I understand that operating from a judgment-free zone is a happy place to be. Allowing myself to view others through their own lenses was another instrumental discovery. Most of the time, people do the best they can with the resources—which are often limited—they have; perfection is but a myth.

The lessons I learned:

- always allow yourself to be vulnerable, as it is in this state that optimal growth is attained
- humility is a virtue of honor—strive to be humble at all costs

- everyone crossing your path is there to fulfill a purpose, good, bad, or indifferent
- embarking on a journey of self-discovery when surrounded by adversity sets a beautiful stage for living a more fulfilled life, which often leads to the healing process
- nothing great comes easy, and if it does, the fruits are only short-lived
- always allow yourself to be an instrument of peace, regardless of the atrocities around you
- stay focused on your quest while searching for your true purpose in life—this revelation will save you in hard times and will provide a great reference point as you navigate through your day to day challenges
- once you find your purpose, strive to execute it at an optimal level
- become that which you were destined to be
- remain true to yourself and others; allow yourself to remain authentic to your values
- aim to have a positive influence on others, but do so with a sense of humility; expect nothing in return
- the good you do will always come back to you ten-fold
- where there is a will, there is always a way—just DO IT
- your inner-strength is greater than you realize—it is insurmountable
- the choices you make will have long-standing effects; choose wisely
- if you deviate from your intended path, forgive yourself and get back on track—nothing remains constant
- appreciate those around you
- have faith in a higher power (God for me)—this deity will always be a part of you and guide you through life
- spend time connecting to your inner-spirit—this regular check-in will speak to you in a gentle voice that sounds loud to your inner ear.

CONCLUSION

Trust that your journey will unfold and end the way it was meant to. Always guard your spirit and keep your head high, even when you have no clue what the next minute will bring. Seize the little moments in life, for they are gifts th continue to give. Your preparedness will influence your ability to receive the see that will grow into sweet fruit. Amidst this dance of life, we are but unique d that make the world complete.

BIOGRAPHY

Serah Muiruri is currently licensed as a certified rehabilitation counselor serving a master level clinician in the ever-progressive field of human services. Serah wor for Nonotuck Resource Associates Inc., a local agency in the state of Massachuset Serah's career began in the early 90s after emigrating from Kenya, her country origin, to the US. In her tenure of service, she has held several positions, servir children and adults with disabilities and often multiple diagnoses, includir Autism Spectrum Disorders, intellectual and cognitive challenges, and acquire brain and trauma injury, among others. Her intrinsic drive to see others succee has influenced Serah's attraction to the field of network marketing, and she h successfully created sizable networks. Additionally, Serah is a trained life coac specializing in neurolinguistics.

Contact Information
Facebook: https://www.facebook.com/serah.muiruri

CHAPTER 25

RESCUE MISSION

By Sheen Marshall

I was on the last of my three jobs for the day. Driving around gives you plenty of time to think about yourself, your situation, and life in general. The previous two days, I had driven for twenty-seven out of the last thirty-two hours. It was brutal and dangerous because I was so tired that I was drifting while driving. I wasn't doing it because I had a love for driving. I was doing it to help make ends meet for my family.

During those long hours behind the wheel, the same thought kept going through my head: "What am I doing wrong?" Crying out to the Lord, as I have done countless times, I couldn't stop asking myself what exactly was I doing wrong that my life would have gotten to this? Life was nowhere near what I had envisioned it would be as a forty-year-old. My family was struggling financially, and we were just barely making ends meet. Our home was in foreclosure, and the business that I launched a few years prior was failing with $85k spent and not a single penny back. It was a terrible situation to be in, and one that I wouldn't want anybody to have to go through. I kept asking myself how a person with a B.S. and Master's Degree could find themselves living this way. Hadn't I done everything I was supposed to? I had followed the system of going to school, getting good grades, and getting a job. But this had led me to being forced to drive twenty-seven out of thirty-two hours just to earn enough money to, hopefully, cover the basic bills. There was that question again: What am I doing wrong?

Sometimes when you're drowning, the Lord will send you a life raft. It's incredible how often I see the life raft thrown to people and they push away—and continue drowning. I refused to allow my story to end like that. never wanted any handouts or freebies; I just wanted a shot. I needed the fire to burn inside me again. I needed to be reborn and to dream again. I needed hope. Fortunately, all of that happened for me in December of 2016. That was the day that an old friend that I hadn't seen in ten years flew into town, without telling me that he was coming, to throw me a life raft. Often, though, we will block or ignore a blessing because it's not wrapped up in the package that we want it to be or expect. So many of us become lost, meaning that we wander through life without a purpose. We haven't found the reason why we are here. I have been fortunate enough to find my purpose, and I'd like to go back a bit now to share with you how I discovered it.

As I look back to those grueling years of driving around as a delivery driver, getting no sleep for little to no money, I always knew that there was something bigger for me out there. I knew that this wasn't my final pit stop. I was still holding out hope that my failed business, a fantasy sports website, would take off, but the grim reality was setting in. I wondered if it was time to finally give up on that dream. But then what? That was the big question. I was previously a teacher for fourteen years, and I was certain that the profession was NOT for me. I disliked it so much that I let my teaching certificate expire because I didn't want it to be an option to fall back on. Leaving that profession, along with starting business, led me to become a delivery driver for multiple companies. I remember showing up for work daily at one of my driving gigs and looking around at the others doing the same thing and wondering how we had all ended up there. There was a man formerly successful in banking, an armed forces veteran, a man who had a successful business and was now in his late seventies, as well as many others, including myself, and we were all forced to deliver delayed luggage for little to no money (that was one of my three delivery jobs). I kept wondering what mistake we had made in life to end up having to do that for a living.

I used to be one of those people who believed that very successful people were always cheating or had some unfair edge over everyone else. Although this may be true SOME of the time, the fact is that very successful people spend lots of time working on themselves. How do they do this? It's called personal development. Amazingly, it's not taught in schools or society in general, NEARLY as much as it should be. When my old friend flew into town to throw me a life raft, what he did was introduce me to personal development. This was through the company I joined, which he was already a part of, that is BIG on personal development. As I started getting deeper into personal development and learning more, it was like an awakening took place within me. I started learning things about myself and others.

What's one of the biggest ways to work on personal development? By reading books, which was one of my BIGGEST weaknesses in life. I never liked to read books. Prior to February of 2020, I hadn't read a book in over fifteen years. As a man with two degrees, it was shameful to admit it. I have heard a saying in the past three years that goes, "success leaves clues."

As I started to observe and follow the people that had the life I wanted, I noticed that a common thing amongst them was the fact that they not only immersed themselves in personal development, but they also read books religiously. While I was sitting stagnant in my company and failing to advance in rank, I began to notice that, often, when someone was being interviewed, at the end of the interview they would be asked, "So what book(s) are you currently reading that you could recommend?" Person after person would quickly be able to call out a book on personal development that they were reading. And I sat there thinking to myself that I was going to beat the system and not follow the playbook by not doing any reading. Meanwhile, I'm looking dumber and dumber.

One of the crucial turning points for me was when I was fortunate enough to be invited to spend the day at the house of the founder of the company that I'm part of. It was on this day that I TRULY learned how much I DIDN'T know. The Bible says, "My people are destroyed for lack of knowledge," and if that ain't the truth, then I don't know what is. The founder of my company talked to a group of us for six hours straight with no break. No matter WHAT the question or topic was, he pulled out a book and was able to flip to a page to answer or address it.

For six hours straight he did this, while I was sitting there saying to myself, "Ho stupid can you really be to think that the people who have the lives that you env all read books constantly, but you think you're going to be the one that makes to where they are without reading at all"? It was at that moment that I realize that my purpose in life was starting to take shape in a manner that I could on have dreamt about.

One of my favorite hip hop artists of all time is a rapper called The Gam He recently released his tenth studio album, which is titled *Born 2 Rap*. He w asked in an interview to explain the title of the album. His answer to the questio has resonated so deeply with me that I recite it often. He said that (paraphrasing "Everybody is born with a purpose. You don't know the point in your life that yo are going to figure that out or when your purpose is going to find you." It too YEARS of struggling, headaches, sadness, and trials for me to find my purpo because it damn sure wasn't wrapped up in the package that I had expected it be.

Nevertheless, I found it and embraced it. I was fortunate enough discover my purpose in life and my destiny. The reason why this chapter is calle "Rescue Mission" is because I must go back and rescue my people. When I sa "my people," I'm not just referring to the black community.

"My people" refers to all those who have realized that they weren't put this earth to struggle to live paycheck to paycheck, be born and die in generation poverty, and not to advance personally or professionally. I believe that God did put us here to struggle. For so many, the daily struggle has become as routine brushing your teeth and tying your shoes. My mission is to take all that I ha learned on my personal development journey and use it to help those who haver learned or been taught these things.

My people are crying out for help, and I am here for them. My missic is to show them that all of their dreams and desires can be attained by investir in themselves. You have LOTS of fight left in you to be the person that God h called you to be, but you must stay in the fight until you realize who you are ar are willing to develop and grow into that person. Maybe you are someone who h yet to find their purpose in life? If that's you, then I say to you Godspeed becau the journey will be WELL WORTH IT. Just keep fighting and it will happen.

ou are reading this and have determined that your purpose is to rescue others as
ell, then our Rescue Mission has just begun, and I look forward to going into
ie trenches with you to help and save as many as we can.

BIOGRAPHY

heen Marshall is a network marketer who spent fourteen years as a school teacher.
His career in network marketing has allowed him to help others find success
n the industry and has also led him to discover his purpose, which is to help
hose who truly want to live and not just be alive. His passions include traveling,
xercising, sports (especially fantasy sports), reading books, and listening to
udios on personal development. He is also an active member of Omega Psi Phi
Fraternity, Inc.

Contact Information

Facebook: https://www.facebook.com/rausheen.marshall

Instagram: https://www.instagram.com/big.sheen05/

CHAPTER 26

WHAT MOST PEOPLE DON'T UNDERSTAND ABOUT NETWORK MARKETING

By Steinar Pettersen

t's now more than two decades since I first became involved in network marketing. The first company that I was introduced to was selling a health product, and after attending the first meeting, I felt very excited about my prospects. I remember talking to my mother about it back then and telling her the things the company had told me during the meeting. It's so easy, I said, the product sells itself, and I'll earn a lot of money. However, I saw myself quitting my job after a couple of weeks because I thought the marketing opportunity would be such an easy and lucrative ride.

Readers who have worked in network marketing will recognize the kind of lies companies feed you when they're trying to enroll you—which I fell for—and the damage done by this sort of misrepresentation is something the network marketing industry must take responsibility for. It's the reason why many marketers all over the world have been overselling in a way that has ultimately

harmed the whole industry and given it a bad reputation. The result is that ne
and innocent marketers struggle at the start of their careers.

During our discussion about the new role, my mum asked me straight ou
"Who do you think is going to buy all these products you are selling?" "You are
I said. "No, I'm not," she replied. She'd already noticed that the product had qui
a small target market, and thought it was unlikely to have a mass appeal.

Looking back, I realized that my mum had already figured out the catc
but I had to figure it out the hard way.

Fueled by courage and enthusiasm, I felt I was moving forward, alwa
looking for my next target, even though I hadn't enrolled in the company. Despi
that, I was dedicated.

Around this time, a friend and his wife came to visit us at our home.
was excited as I started to tell our guests about the company and the produc
and how I was expecting to make BIG money with almost no effort. But m
friend interrupted me, saying, "Steinar, I've already enrolled with the compar
you're talking about." Surprised, I asked him how it was going. He told me th
he had so far failed to enroll anybody or shift any product at all, despite having
basement full of products that he'd paid for. His wife suggested that he try to se
some of it, but he said she could have a go at doing it because he didn't want t
We all had a good laugh about that.

That proved to be a fateful conversation for me, and you could say th
my good friend "saved" me from network marketing at that time. After learnir
about his experience, it dawned on me that this was far from an easy way
make lots of money with little effort. I think it's because of the way that the id
is sold to many freshly recruited marketers, as it was to me, that most of the
don't understand why they end up struggling with their business and lose mone
They're given an unrealistic idea of what's involved and think they've joined
network where they don't have to do anything but watch the money come rollir
in. But guess what? Network marketing is hard work, like any other business.
you want to succeed in your career, you have to put in the hours.

Looking back, I think I have always been a dedicated guy, someone wh
easily gets excited about new things. I remember getting my first real permane
job at sixteen while I was still studying to become a mechanic. I vividly recall th

ay I drove out to the farm on my moped and applied for the job in person. It involved taking care of the animals, feeding them, gathering eggs, and milking the cows during the weekends and vacations. I was thrilled when I got the job and felt so proud when I was able to tell my parents. It was through that job that I learned to take responsibility at an early age. At that time, I was so dedicated to agriculture that I thought I was going to be a farmer. However, after finishing studying mechanics three years later, I already knew that the one thing I wasn't going to be was a farmer.

So, I got a job as a mechanic, working with pressured systems: first steam boilers, and then pressure air systems. Because I'm from Norway and come from the area known as the country's "Oil Capital," I had the opportunity to work offshore in the North Sea on oil installations as a technician on the air and firefighting systems. I had other missions, too, working as a course instructor when our company oversaw the gas contingency onboard. In total, I worked offshore for around fifteen years, an experience I value very highly. Then, about ten years ago, I moved into the sales department of the company. I had a flying start and made a new record for sales. Everything was good, and everybody was happy.

However, a few years later, there was a crisis in the oil industry, and everything came to a halt. Sales levels dropped dramatically, and my boss changed the rules about sales payments. Under the new regime, all sales personnel would only be paid for the sales they closed during personal sales meetings and not when orders came *through the house*. As I was selling the most expensive products, I was the biggest loser in the new system. I was unable to make anywhere near the same level of sales through meetings as before, so my income fell sharply, and before long, I found myself frozen out of the company.

You can imagine how my self-esteem plummeted. I was at rock-bottom. It was then that I decided to leave sales for good and never return. So, I got a job working as a technical manager in one of the biggest greenhouses in Norway.

Six months later, in January 2017, my upline Frank gave me a call out of the blue. He asked me if I would like to come to a meeting the following Sunday. I said I would if I didn't have to sell anything, and he assured me that it was just an opportunity that he wanted to offer me. So, I went along to the meeting and sat through the presentation. It all sounded so good that I got super-excited again, and agreed to sign on as a customer, although, in my heart, I really wanted sign up as a marketer, as well. However, I remained somewhat skeptical, as I'd lo some money on other scams previously.

Consequently, I told Frank that I needed some time to consider signing u as a marketer but would stay in touch. I hit on the idea of enlisting some of m friends to join me at the next meeting, thinking that I'd wait to see their reactio if they joined, so would I. If they didn't, then neither would I. I felt that th would act as a sort of insurance. But I made a big mistake; I revealed to my frien what the meeting was about.

In Norway, network marketing has a terrible reputation, and most peop don't want to get involved. Norway is one of the wealthiest countries in th world, so people usually don't have to take a job if they don't want to. There's welfare safety net for the unemployed, although it certainly won't make anyo wealthy. However, right now, like most people, I'm not sure how long this safe net will last after the coronavirus pandemic. I've heard people in Norway sayir on the news that they've only got a few kroner in their bank accounts because th new payment system designed by the government to support people during th pandemic isn't yet working as planned.

Anyway, after I told my friends what the meeting was about, they bail out, and I did the same. Some days later, my upline called me again and said th he'd heard that the meeting was canceled. I confirmed that it was and told hi that I was still skeptical. But Frank didn't take no for an answer, saying that he w sure I'd regret it if I didn't enroll. I didn't like what he said but ended up enrolli anyway, and also enrolled one of my friends who was willing to take a chance.

Once I'd enrolled and started working, my old dedication for netwo marketing returned, and I found that I really liked the new company. Nevertheles I remember finding many excuses not to pick up the phone and start recruitir new people. At the time, I didn't have the right skills to do it successfully.

It's worth mentioning here that, in my experience, this is also somethir people starting out don't fully understand about network marketing—to do th work successfully, you need the proper training and the tools.

I soon started to join new meetings and began taking part in trainir sessions. I remember we had a visit from one of the company presidents during

eeting. He asked the room, who was willing to leave their comfort zone. I was
he first to raise my hand, and he asked me to come up on the stage. I remember
him telling me about some of the events that were planned. It was profoundly
exciting, but he didn't understand why I thought all this was such a big deal.

Not long after that, I attended my first event in Torino, Italy. It was a
fantastic experience, with a far bigger crowd in attendance than I had ever imagined
possible. Eric Worre was conducting the training, and I could relate to everything
he said. As Eric was lifting us all up with his step training, I was so fired up that
I dared myself into doing something I would never usually do. During a break in
the training session, I was chatting to a musician from a band that I like, when
Worre started walking through the audience. I thought to myself, if he passes me,
I'm going to give him a handshake. And that's precisely what happened. Later,
Frank said that I was the only person who had successfully managed to divert Eric
from his usual routine at such events.

I must say that it was at this training event that I think Eric Worre changed
my life. I really want to thank you for that, Eric!

After the event, my career suddenly kickstarted—I went from Level 2 to
Level 5 within a month. I remember being so full of energy that I sometimes had
to let off steam by screaming in my car as I was driving along. Seeing my success,
the company invited me to a leadership conference in Vienna, where I met the
founder of the company.

My motivation to work was at its peak, plus I had great mentors who helped
me get better at the job. We all put a lot of time into it. That reminds me to thank
my lovely wife, Siv, who patiently put up with me spending so much time on
developing the business. From time to time, she joked that the new business was
my new wife.

Even when Siv and I were on a holiday in Spain, Eric Worre was with me on
the sunbed, not physically, but in my ear and on the screen. I was learning how to
recruit twenty people in thirty days. While I was training, I also started to figure
out how I could put my own twist on the job. I began preparing for presentations,
calling my father from Spain, and instructing him how to do a drawing for me
that would make it easier to get my message across to people at meetings. By the

end of the holiday, I had completed the training, which was like getting a monkey off my back. I found I was genuinely enjoying the business and having fun.

Many people don't understand that an important aspect of network marketing is the support you get from others. Plus, you can start your own business from home, and no formal educational qualifications are needed if you're willing to work hard. As I see it, one of the biggest problems facing the industry is that many people aren't ready for that level of responsibility and hard work. Several factors can get in their way, and the biggest is the fear of rejection. Many starting out are simply not adequately prepared for this, so when the fifth person says no, they give up. There's an easy remedy to this problem: if upline give newly enrolled people more time to do the training step-by-step, then I'm convinced that many more would succeed. It seems likely to me that, after the coronavirus is contained, people will be more receptive to the business and the network marketing concept.

Sadly, the network marketing business I worked for closed in Norway about two years ago. It gave a lot of people an excuse to quit. I didn't quit. Instead, I focused on getting more training. In fact, during the family's celebration of my mum's seventieth birthday in Italy, I was still doing live training courses with Frazer Brookes on my cell phone. Thanks, Frazer, for all the great training sessions and the books!

I'd like to send a special thank you to Matt Morris, who has supported me daily with great emails, live training, and other videos. He's always happy and full of energy, and I want to thank him for all the times he's lifted me up when the going was tough, and I wasn't producing any results.

I'll sign off by saying, because of network marketing, I am now back in sales.

BIOGRAPHY

Steinar Pettersen comes from Sandnes in Norway. He is an entrepreneur and business coach. After starting out as a mechanical engineer working offshore in the North Sea for the oil industry, he has since enjoyed a long and successful career in network marketing. He has participated in many network marketing training events hosted by industry luminaries such as Eric Worre, Tony Robbins, Frazer Brookes, and Matt Morris. Steinar is also the founder of a video production company. He's now dedicated to helping people succeed in their network marketing business.

Contact Information

Facebook: https://www.facebook.com/steinar.pettersen.98

Instagram: https://www.instagram.com/steinarsin/

Website: https://www.futurehomeoffice.com/

CHAPTER 27

FROM GO TO WOE . . . AND BACK AGAIN

By Stephen Davis

I was born at the bottom of the world with sixty-six million sheep and three million people, and pastures and scenery as far as the eye could see—my home, New Zealand.

A beautiful place and at the time when parents left their kids by themselves, ars were packed like sardines, and you left home without locking the doors . . . ell, scratch that last bit, I grew up in one of the lowest economic places in New ealand, and if you didn't lock the door, then you would probably lose that door nong other things.

Devoid of any cell phones, internet, or video games—in fact, there as barely a TV with two channels—we made our own fun, created our own dventures.

My childhood was full of life and mischievousness. I belonged to a neration of kids who were left to their own devices for hours on end and, as you ay imagine, did everything you can think of.

We turned the house into a bomb zone, the coffee table into a sled, we en practiced flying off the roof, jumping off rooftops and through windows numerous houses, played tag around glass doors, somersaulted over concrete fences, let strange kids in our homes, lit matches, and firecrackers inside, made our neighborhood block into our "Olympics" park, turned our park trees into makeshift climbing walls, and crawled underground into partly-laid pipes by local authorities with nothing but a torch and courage.

I broke things, lost things, messed up things, climbed everything you can imagine while safeguarding my explorer spirit.

It was not surprising that I ended up with battle scars and in trouble several times. But I wouldn't trade it for anything, for it made my childhood memorable and led to an adventurous life.

I developed a knack for losing things. I lost my school term bus pass regularly and ended up running to and from school daily. I became extra fit, but it wasn't so great when the bus driver who often gave me free rides, asked my mother why I was running all the time? Ouch!

I was also "famous" for repeating the same mistakes. How many times I spent kneeling on the lounge floor with my siblings, saying sorry to mum and promising never to repeat the behavior, only to do it all over again the next week. The perils of such cyclic behavior came to haunt me later.

I harbored a few insecurities. Growing up with mixed heritage, I didn't fit into either culture and there was prejudice too. My parents constantly fought, and this meant that from as young as a preschooler, I was often the barrier between whether one got hurt or not.

We moved cities at a key time, which meant that I had to start new friendships and adapt while tackling the adolescent worries of pimples, hair growth, and low self-esteem issues.

In my new city, on New Zealand's beautiful South Island, my high school science teacher Mrs. Metcalfe, who upon seeing an insecure young man, said "Stephen, you have a beautiful smile." To date, I am grateful to her for the positive reinforcement she gave me.

Sometimes the simplest comments can leave the most profound impact, positive or negative. Since then, most people often notice and compliment my smile.

Being "famous" as a child can be far more fun than painful. But as an adult it entails entirely different things.

Remember when I said I was known to repeat the same mistakes?

I led my life by following meticulously carved plans. I was striving to fulfill my vision. I was married, owned a house, had a growing family, and a career to see me through to retirement. I had money saved and money growing, all was going according to the plan.

I was leading a life that most people dream of.

But as fate would have it, in a short amount of time, I lost it all. I came home from work one day to find the house half-empty; my wife of ten years was gone with the kids. I was forced to sell the house and watched half a million dollars disappear down the drain. With my career finished, my reputation hit rock bottom. Some "friends" and "loved ones" turned a blind eye while muttering "God bless," "All the best," etc.

I felt that the Universe was out to get me and I crumbled under surmounting pressure. Blaming God, the Universe, everyone, and everything else, I retreated deep into my shell. My health plunged, my hair greyed, my weight ballooned, and for the first time in my adult life, the future looked bleak.

The pain was so great, the depression and numbness so debilitating that I struggled to even leave my parents' home, which I had returned to for some respite.

I was barely alive, let alone doing anything else. My life had fallen apart dramatically.

But, lost in the middle of this perfect storm, I found a way through. And no matter what you encounter, I assure you there will always be a way through for you too.

Here's what I discovered, and may it help you in your time of need and guide you toward the life that you seek.

Key 1: Take Time Before You Are Forced to Take the Time

I remember the night that was the culmination of everything that occurred. I had no home, not even my parents'. Out under the stars at the beach, I contemplated my life and the possible future that lay ahead of me.

I had not pondered so deep in decades or asked any existential questions. It's no wonder I was a mess.

It is better to take a deep, hard look at your life before you have no oth
choice than to do so.

Key 2: Reach Out; Save Yourself Unnecessary Pain

At times, a third person and their objective perspective could become a k
difference between a life mended or one torn asunder.

Before I slept, I phoned some people who played heartfelt roles in m
life, and in doing so, it stopped me from doing anything stupid; stupidity whic
would have further derailed my life.

Key 3: You Can Change

Being on my own, with nothing, going nowhere, I had plenty of time to thin
During that time, I had a deep realization.

It didn't matter wrong had been done to me, and how bad the situation i
it did not have to dictate the rest of my life. I could change it; the power was
my hands.

The realization freed me, and I began to let go. I was free to rebuild anew
For the first time in ever so long, I slept peacefully.

Key 4: Look and Listen Carefully for Life's Clues; Learn early, Save Pain Later

Life has a way of sorting us all out—call it God, a higher power, or the Univers
I started recognizing patterns in my life; different people, places, and tim
but repeated situations, with an almost déjà vu precision.

I thought, "How could this keep happening?" "What was the connection

I then had an epiphany—these were situations that I hadn't learned fror
situations I had not resolved properly. It hit me like a ton of bricks.

In hindsight, I could see that throughout my life, I was "famous" f
repeating the same pattern of dealing with situations. Consequently, I hit th
same insurmountable walls over and over again.

It was clear how each similar situation became increasingly worse, leadir
up to the hardest time in my life.

I created a recipe for disaster by putting a band-aid on deep wounds and carrying on, until my life fell apart.

Key 5: Your Life Is 100 Percent Your Responsibility

I gained a new perspective and was shaken out of a victim mentality— "Why me?" or "How unfair!" Instead, I replaced it with a new understanding that my life was my own responsibility, no one else's. Soon, the questions changed to, "Why not me?" or "Life can be unfair, so what?"

It was the kick in the proverbial backside I needed, and I was so grateful to finally learn the lesson.

You can let life do you in, or you can take life and make it happen for you.

Key 6: Clear the Rubble of Your Life

It's one thing to get through something, it's a whole another to get over it. Throughout my life, I recall many situations where I held grudges for such long times. It was during the hardest time of my life that I felt the full weight of holding onto those grudges. I could feel the pull of those grudges dragging me down.

I lived for two years in such a damaged way that it compelled me to think of the finiteness of life. I came out, and adopted the motto, "One life, live it fully, have no regrets."

I properly processed what happened, felt the pain, forgave, let go, and moved on. Notice how I didn't say hide or forget the pain. If you try and do this, the pain has a nasty habit of resurfacing again, in unattractive ways, and at embarrassing moments.

I decided never would I let any situation ever cause me to dwell on it so long again and I haven't.

Ask yourself would you rather spend fifty years or more getting over something, blaming others, and being right . . . or let it go and live your best life?

Time does not care if you mope around for five minutes or fifty years. It ticks on, indifferently.

Now unless you know that you have an extra life or two up your sleeve . . . save yourself unnecessary life-sapping energy.

Key 7: Step Forward, Do Something Constructive with Your Life

From the worst soil grew a bud of hope. Within a week, I had a roof over my head, my kids with me, and shortly after, my new employment secured. I then began to rebuild the shambles of my life with a new foundation.

I took counseling, gained inspiration online and offline, and connected with people globally. I watched, listened, learned and grew, spent time discovering who I was, and doing things I loved.

A lifetime of developing an unhealthy mindset takes some time to dismantle.

I did not shy away from asking difficult questions to myself and others, for I knew it was needed to overcome the hurdles of a regressive mindset. Find your inner child and be courageous to give new things a go. In doing so, you will stretch yourself, grow, and discover the whole new *you*.

Remember, no will always remain a no if you choose to do nothing. So as you do, and give yourself a chance of being the best *you*.

FINAL THOUGHTS

Why do some harvest their true potential, find success, and be financially well off, while many others continue to struggle? It's the barrier in their mind that gets in the way.

So . . .
Key 1 - *Take time before you are forced to take the time*
Key 2 - *Reach out; save yourself unnecessary pain*
Key 3 - *You can change*
Key 4 - *Look and listen carefully for life's clues; learn early, save pain later*
Key 5 - *Life is 100 percent your responsibility*
Key 6 - *Clear the rubble of your life*
Key 7 - *Step forward, do something constructive with your life*

Be that person who considers things most won't, take action where most don't. and you'll gain the life that most miss out on.

nd Where Am I Now?

Healthy, fit, in a loving relationship, a great dad with wonderful kids, an author, successful businessman, and moving quickly toward fulfilling my lifetime vision f being a global mentor, trainer, and inspiration.

Like nothing will stop me, let nothing stop you.

Break preconceived ideas, notions, and a lifetime mindset. Let go of pain nd the things of the past.

Remove the barriers, build afresh, and abundant success will follow.

BIOGRAPHY

tephen Davis is a mentor, coach, and successful networker. He is passionate out helping others to succeed, inspire, and impact their lives. He works out f his home in the beautiful garden city of Christchurch, New Zealand. He likes ending his summers camping and adventuring locally and abroad with his arling and their four children. If you look closely, you might find him dancing mong the treetops . . . but not too closely, he has already fallen once and broken oth wrists.

Contact Information

acebook: https://www.facebook.com/StephenJDavisOne/
nstagram: https://www.instagram.com/2dreambelievelive/

CHAPTER 28

JUST DECIDE - THERE IS NO OTHER OPTION

By Steve Eastin

W hat happens when you finally decide that failure and living an average life is not an option?

What's holding you back?

Is it your age? That's only a number.

Your ego? Do you think that you can do it on your own?

Your choices? Okay, maybe you haven't made the best of choices, but you ave to let that go.

Your past? Let it go.

Your mistakes? We all make them; just let them go.

Your financial situation? There are a lot of ways to make money—take a sk once in a while.

The negative people around you? Find new people.

Your own negative thoughts? Start creating positive ones.

The haters? This is my favorite one—prove them wrong.

Easier said than done, right?

My journey to mastering the above started when I was 11 years old. My om and dad were entrepreneurs at heart, and they worked extremely hard. I watched them go to work, buy an apartment complex, create businesses, and build relationships.

Around the 11th year of my life, my dad made a statement that has stuck with me ever since: "You will never get rich working for someone else." This indicates that proverbial turning point (a noun referring to a decisive change in situation, especially one with beneficial results).

Dad led by example; his actions said what words could not. In the book *Rich Dad Poor Dad* by Robert T. Kiyosaki, the Rich Dad describes my father to a T, but I did not read that book until later in life. It wasn't until reading the book and taking stock of what I know now that I realized that my dad and mom were actually mentors and teachers.

Dad and mom eventually fired their bosses and continued with the investments and businesses. They were true entrepreneurs. Unfortunately, my dad died in his semi-retirement at the age of 44 in a small plane crash in Alaska while enjoying a hunting expedition. I was 19 at the time. Dad was on his way to millionaire status, but Death and Destiny had different plans for him.

After watching my parents when I was 11-years-old, I decided to get a jump on things and start my own lawn mowing service. I made some contacts, lined up some customers, and away I went. The money was good until the weather turned cold. The money after that came in the form of payment for household chores. It was not as good, but there was still money coming in. I always had multiple jobs throughout high school, but nothing significant.

When I hit 20-years-old, a new turning point occurred when I married my high school sweetheart. I convinced her that I would give her everything she desired because I would be a millionaire by my 44th birthday. I promised that our lives would be remarkable, worthy of attention. Unfortunately, I never achieved my goal. My theory is that I started to work for other people, helping to make their dreams come true instead of my own.

I worked in a mailroom and as a bartender. I still mowed lawns, and was a cashier at Target. There were also some purifier sales and a job as a sales representative later in life. This pattern continued, allowing me to support my wife and enjoy the birth of our daughter. We lived in luxury—kidding! It was a two-bedroom apartment where the cockroaches were so big that we named them

ıd called them our pets. Through it all, I knew that if I kept working at these
ıbs, it would soon pay off.

I worked my way up from that mailroom to customer support; at least I
as moving up. It still felt as if something was missing. I knew that I was not
ıswering my calling, nor was I keeping the promise I had made to my wife. I
ıd this burning desire to help people and be in a position of authority, so I quit
retty much all of the jobs I had, including the customer service position. Next,
decided to be a police officer at the age of 30—it was always something I had
anted to do.

Supporting two children now, I graduated from the police academy—from
hich, I might add, several people were pretty surprised that I had (take that,
ıters). I first became a reserve officer, then a paid dispatcher, and I was eventually
worn into the patrol division. Trust me—I could write an entire book on that
8-year tour of duty, but I'll save that for another day. I will, however, tell you
ıat it changed my life.

Believe it or not, my pattern of multiple jobs continued during my police
ıreer. While working as an officer, I started a trucking company, a construction
ımpany, and a trailer refurbishing company, all of which were operating at the
ıme time at one point. I managed employees, did the accounting, spent time at
ıe various locations, swung a hammer—you name it, I did it all while performing
ıy police duties to a high standard. I never slept, but by God, I was going to be
millionaire by the age of 44. My future was bright. The money was pouring in.

All was good until the economy crashed. I will spare you the details, but
ıit just happened. I lost everything in a blink of an eye: savings accounts, toys,
ısinesses, and the house. And then the ultimate happened: bankruptcy.

If you have ever experienced the feeling of not knowing where you and
ıur family are going to live after you have uprooted them from everything they
ıew, it cannot be explained, but it sucked!

We lost the home on our 60 acres, but we were blessed to find a townhome
ı our community that served its purpose over the next few years.

During that time, I chose not to quit but stayed more positive and more
ıtermined than ever to succeed.

The bankruptcy taught me that I was doing it all wrong. Though I w
working extremely hard, I had decided to assume the responsibility and blame f
my situation.

I truly felt that God had put me in that position to let me know th
striving to be a millionaire was about nothing but greed. And something was st
missing, but I could not figure out what it was.

I got my real estate license in 2009 while still a police officer, continuing t
pattern of working multiple jobs, and it has worked out well over time. I was ba
in the financial fight, but unbeknownst to me, I was still in the proverbial rat rac

These two professions began to take their toll on me, becoming mo
demanding and time-consuming. There was no such thing as sleep, family tim
or vacations. Unfortunately, I became more selfish than before, which led to
downhill spiral for the worse. I started to become a recluse, I did not want
spend time with anybody, and I just stopped being me. I was not the kind
person others wanted to be around.

One day while on patrol, I received a text message from my daughter. In
she laid out the truth. She advised me that I could do anything, that she and t
rest of the family wanted me back, and that I should retire. This was interestir
because I was the type of person that you could not tell what to do, nor wou
I take someone else's advice. It was a brave thing my daughter had done. Than
God, I listened to what she said. It struck my soul, and I knew she was rig
because I felt at peace.

Ironically, my commander called me into the office later that day to see wh
I had decided about my schedule for the following year. The schedule had bee
written on a whiteboard in his office. I found myself staring at it long enough th
my commander asked me for my decision once more. I knew I had to save m
relationship with my family, and I had to fix me. I looked at my commander ar
told him I was giving him a week's notice. He stated, "You're f****n kidding me

After we determined that I wasn't kidding, I agreed to a two-week stay
assist with training my replacement. After the two weeks, my agency gave me
fantastic retirement party, and I left law-enforcement. I am very grateful for m
agency, and I would not change anything about my law enforcement career.
believe it was a journey that I needed to take.

To all of the family members of men and women in law-enforcement, the military, and first responders: thank you so much for what you do, I know what involved, you are special, and I pray for all of you every day.

Holy crap! Now, what would I do with no job, very little savings, a small 01(k), and no real estate deal in sight? I guess you could say that I took a leap f faith.

I was pretty much in survival mode for the next year or so. My savings were ot big, and the IRS loved me. I searched for my next turning point and what I ad been missing.

The answer was simple: I just dropped the ego and asked for help. By 1at time, I had surrounded myself with some amazing mentors who gave me 1e advice to read books, take pride in myself, invest in some self-development asses, my mind, my financial education, and my training, so I did. What do you now? They were right. Most importantly, I devoted myself to God and stopped oubting him and the power of prayer.

I finally understand that you can't always do things on your own and it is kay to ask for help. I've learned about financial strategies and that relationships e more important than anything. It taught me how to create a focus board and alues list and to visualize my goals and create affirmations. Trust me on this one: rite it down, or it won't happen.

I now know my destiny, and I have found my core purpose in life. Life is o longer about my wants, needs, or material possessions. It is about the wants 1d needs of other people. It is about helping people to become leaders. It is about elping people succeed in helping others invest in themselves. It is about helping eople to create a lifestyle of their own that they can control. The bottom line is, needed to figure out how to become a leader for the right reasons before I could elp others do the same.

To all who are reading this book, decide that failure and living an average fe is not an option, and age is just a number. Start your positive transformation day. You can do it. I believe in you.

To my wife: I have not quite reached millionaire status yet, but thank you r being so remarkable and never giving up on me, no matter what.

BIOGRAPHY

Steve Eastin has been in the public eye for over 20 years. He has worked with thousands of people in different aspects of their lives and is deemed by friends as a successful life coach. His educational experience consists of ethics training, crisis intervention, crisis and business negotiations, and leadership and self development. Steve is a successful entrepreneur with growing businesses. He is married to Brenda since 1986 and is blessed with a son, Danny, a daughter, Amanda, a son-in-law, Calvin, and granddaughter, Indiana Cree.

Contact Information
Facebook: https://www.facebook.com/profile.php?id=100009492462937

CHAPTER 29

PERCEPTION IS EVERYTHING

By Syen Yap

Have you ever wondered why some people seem to have so much good *luck* in their lives with everything always going their way? They just appear so positive and bad things never seem to happen to them.

I'm embarrassed to admit it, but sometimes I want to hate them, or at least el green with jealousy. It's not fair, right? Well, it's always been a mystery to me, I decided to try to discover if some people are just born lucky. And, maybe, ong the way, I might figure out how to get luck on my side.

I came from a normal family with four siblings. However, my parents got vorced when I was in secondary school—when I was about fifteen years old. A t of people might think that might not be a great situation, especially during ur growing-up journey.

But today, I'm actually glad about that event; we children no longer had to ep listening to the arguments or endure the hostile atmosphere at home every ay, when we came back from school. I now think it's good that both my parents ok the next step, so that the changes allowed them to live much better lives.

Yes, it was challenging for me and my siblings when our parents separated. followed my mom, and my siblings followed my dad. I took this path because

I felt that I understood why my mom made the hard decision, and I wanted to at least be by her side. My siblings and I communicated by letters, with me on going back once a week during the weekends to visit them.

There was one time when my youngest brother forgot to bring the house key, so, after he came back from school at around one in the afternoon, he had no choice (without a phone) but to sit by the front of the house, under the hot sun, waiting for another sibling with a key to arrive around seven in the evening. After a couple of hours, the next-door neighbour realized the situation and allowed him to wait inside their house, while he waited for the other sibling to return later that evening.

When I learned this, I felt so sad that my younger brother had to go through that. However, there wasn't a single time I blamed my parents or the divorce for it. I decided back then to always believe that things happen for a reason.

I am proud to say that, having gone through this life-test while growing up, all my siblings became very independent and mature compared to their friends of the same age. We rarely asked for help from a parent unless it was absolutely necessary. We monitored our own education, deciding on the courses we would take by ourselves. Even then, all of use understood that each person has to craft the life they want by themselves—that we are all responsible for our futures and no one else.

Fast forward to my life as an adult, and you might agree with me that my difficult growing-up journey had a purpose behind it. My attitude about life back then has now come full circle, and I still make decisions on the basis of my belief that our responsibility in life is to be the type of person that is a blessing to others.

My first job was in the hotel industry as a sales executive, followed by a second in the exhibition industry. Within these two entirely different environments, I was blessed to have a supervisor who really took care of me, always fighting for me, and earning my goodwill. I discovered that, as with growing up, there are workplace politics that threaten to drag us down. However, I instinctively chose not to participate in them, simply because such entanglements create so many problems—and there is never any gain.

Here are a few examples: Once, I shared this practice of positive perception with one of my colleagues, Joseph. I told him that I thought I must be a true

essed person because I had so many great people around me. He replied, "That's
ecause you always have an attitude that everyone appreciates—you always look
 everything in such a positive way. So, all the negatives seem of such little
nportance that you cease to care about them."

Then, a year ago, I became involved in my first network marketing company.
t that time, our team was not very strong. It seemed as though many people were
ninking that they would wait until the team grew stronger or the brand become
opular before they would commit to joining because they thought it would then
e much easier for them.

But a voice inside whispered to me, "Why don't we become the *pioneers* and
nake it work when others won't? Isn't it challenges like this that create the greatest
opportunities for us to learn and grow as people? The best memories we have in
fe are often of overcoming the challenges that, at the time, felt like the most
ifficult. But I say that those are the times when there is the greatest opportunity
o build a strong foundation.

And, although our team was small, I'm so grateful that we had a great leader
ith the long-term vision of building something strong together. How grateful I
n to be to be part of such a team!

Then, in early 2020, the COVID-19 pandemic arrived—the virus that took
vay thousands and thousands of human lives. People everywhere are suffering
ecause of the coronavirus. Countries are in lock-down, with people asked by
neir leaders to stay at home. The world has been forced to freeze all economic,
ocial, and physical development activities. Many people are genuinely worried
hether this will be the end of the world, as the impact of the virus seems greater
an any other event in human history. And it's happening globally. Will we
urvive? And if we survive, how will the world function in the future?

Yet, a few months on, the great news is that there are many signs that
other Earth is healing herself. Plus, there are other positive outcomes—like
e decrease of air pollution from factories and autos. We have better air quality.
nd not only that, but the quality of water has shown significant improvement
. Venice, as well as in rivers in India. Wild animals have appeared in groups to
claim their territory, and the Earth's ozone layer is healing by itself.

But does this remind us of how much damage we have done to our Moth
Earth for the sake of so-called progress and economic gain? Can the pandemic b
seen as a warning, a lesson from Mother Earth to force us to stop and think deep
about what we have done with her kindness? Have we wondered why COVID-1
has spread so quickly and lethally amongst humanity, forcing us to stay at home f
the safety of ourselves and others, while the animal kingdom remains untouche
You could say that the animals are now claiming their "freedom" back from us.

Maybe we should be paying greater respect to Mother Nature? As human
we claim to be the most intelligent among all the living species on our planet y
when we look at the bigger picture, we see that we only play a small role in th
greater scheme of things.

Perhaps Mother Nature is reminding us to be more than just takers, selfish
squandering her bountiful resources? By focusing only on our personal gain, ha
we truly forgotten that we should also give back and show our care for her?

Today, I sit quietly in appreciation of the situation. This pandemic ma
be the biggest opportunity for humankind to grow and gain that it has ever ha
It may be saving us from the day of reckoning that will come at the end of th
world. I believe that, if we wake up and take better care our planet, we might sav
ourselves from utter extinction.

If I may, I would love to share with you an idea of mine that comes fro
the center of my soul; today, globally, I believe there are two types of people facir
this pandemic:

Type 1 – Focusing on the virus, blaming others as to why it is happenin
while the virus continues spreading due to the stress created by peoples' consta
complaining.

Type 2 – Accept the situation and take it as a challenge, looking for
solution while feeling grateful for being safe and healthy.

Please don't misunderstand me—I'm not asking you to be oblivio
to the fact that bad things happen in life. Of course, they do. And it's okay
acknowledge that we do not know how the future will turn out. But my life h
taught me that what matters is how you choose to look at things: Do you percei
certain situations, like the pandemic, as "Bad Luck" or "A Great Challenge"?

I wish to share with you the secret that has helped me in my life: If we decide to take up the power residing within us that comes from choosing how we respond to life's challenges, that directly affects how we feel inside. Instead of choosing to be a victim, we can choose to live as great students, constantly pushing ourselves to rise above the expectations of our great Professor and earn the best grade we can. I believe that power lays in the way we look at any given situation and our mindset affects the consequences resulting from the actions we choose to take.

It begins with your choice of not *what* but *how* you choose to believe. It's all a matter of perception. For instance, I choose to believe that things happen for a reason, and that outcomes are a result of what we did or failed to do in the past. Think about it this way—that life may be testing you, giving you an opportunity to begin to transform yourself into who you're meant to be— a better version of yourself!

Yes, I could have chosen to blame my parents about not giving us the best lifestyle during my childhood. Yes, I could choose to complain about why my career path has had so many ups and downs and difficulties. Yes, I could choose to blame others for this pandemic. But there is something that I know within the depths of my soul: None of these behaviours will serve me well. None of these beliefs will change the situation for the better, and all such negative emotions only hurt me.

But if I *choose* to accept the situation, switching my way of thinking—my perception—gives me the *courage* to face all these wonderful challenges with positivity. Because, in my experience, challenges usually mean an opportunity to grow and become a better version of myself.

Remember, as human beings, we do not have the power to control what will happen. But we do have the power to choose how we respond to life's challenges by deliberately aiming our intent towards the outcomes that we want to achieve.

My friend, please be grateful for whatever happens in life. Every event is a meaningful piece in the grand puzzle of life, one that helps us paint the story of our lives that we can recall again and again when telling it to our great grandchildren. When we inspire them with our courage to make the best of life's challenges, we are seeding the power of positive perception into their minds and ensuring that their world will be even better than ours.

BIOGRAPHY

Syen Yap is a professional executive in the exhibition and network marketing industries. Challenging career environments have built her tough and resilient character that always looks for solutions to problems through a positive mindset. Her life experience and positive attitude in life has successfully helped her create an influencing power over more than one hundred people, who have been inspired to change their way of thinking. Syen loves adventure and enjoys outdoor sports such as diving, riding, hiking, and camping. By the age of twenty-six, she has traveled to more than ten countries. Her passions include inspiring others to live with gratitude and living her life to the fullest by sharing her story and lifestyle.

Contact Information
Facebook: https://www.facebook.com/si.yen.14

CHAPTER 30

PULLING YOUR OWN WEIGHT

By Toni Catchings

I remember when I first started playing sports. All my grade school friends were playing soccer, so I wanted to play too. Soccer came easily to me, and I found that I loved the game. As I got older, I became interested in playing for a better team in a more competitive league. The team I was hoping to play with was highly successful. To join the new team, I had to try out. The coaches would have all the aspiring players perform the same tasks, and then they would pick the best performers. I remember watching a tryout so that I could figure out what was required. I realized that, to be successful, I needed to practice, practice, and practice again. My dad would go with me to a local football field and help me practice. Finally, the time for tryouts arrived, and I made the team. I continued to play with this team for the next five years.

The team coach was a little intense. He had really high expectations of his players. For instance, if your uniform shirt came untucked during a game and you didn't fix it immediately, he subbed you out of the game. Practices were always challenging. We started every practice with a one-and-a-half to two miles timed run. Then, we had to complete one hundred sit-ups, followed by jumping rope for a specific number of successful jumps. Once everyone had completed this,

then practice began. At the end of practice, we always finished with both fif
and one hundred yard sprints. At this time in my life, I REALLY hated runnin
But I knew that if I wanted to play with this team, it was just something that
had to do, whether I liked it or not. I was learning how to carry my own weigh
although I didn't even know it at the time. I did know that I was definitely pa
of a TEAM, and that we were working and playing for and with each other bot
on and off the field.

When I was nineteen, the team was invited to represent the United Stat
in an invitational international soccer tournament in China. Back then, the
were no U.S. women's national or Olympic soccer teams. We won most of ou
games, but we also had a tie with China and a loss to Australia. We still qualifie
for the semi-finals and made it through to the finals. But, of course, who did w
have to play in the finals? Australia again! We had already lost to them once. Di
we honestly think we could beat them?

I remember feeling super-nervous when the final game started. We made
to half-time, and the score was still tied nil-nil. I remember seeing my teammates d
things that I had never seen them do before during that game. The determinatio
that we had to come back and beat this team was INTENSE! Everyone on th
team took care of business. When the final whistle blew, my teammates and I we
exhausted by the supreme effort that we'd put into beating our opponents, but th
feeling of accomplishment was overwhelming. Final score: USA one, Australia n

Now, as an adult, I realize that the coach pushed us so much to make su
that everyone could carry their own weight during a game. We would all be ab
to push through and continue to play until the whistle blew at the end of th
game.

I have another soccer championship memory, where I did not carry my ow
weight. It was during another final game to determine the best team in the count
for our age group. We were tied with the other team, and they had control of th
ball. The next play involved the player I was responsible for marking. I rememb
thinking to myself that she would mess up, and I could relax a little. My po
decision to relax and not give it my full effort changed the game; she made th
right play and did it well because I wasn't challenging her. I underestimated h
will to win and her ability. Within the next few minutes, that team scored a go

KNEW it was my fault. We never came back from that. The other team won
 те championship. I had failed my teammates and myself. I remember that poor
зcision to this day. My lack of effort let down eighteen other people and all our
ns. Even now, years later, I often wish that I could go back in time and have that
юment back—and make a different decision. Of course, that's impossible, and
must live with it.

Life continued, and I found myself divorced at the age of twenty-seven
ter five-and-a-half years of marriage. This utterly crushed me. I felt ashamed of
те situation because I felt as though I had failed. I was not proud of having to
dmit that we could not work things out. Now, I had to figure out how to carry
ту own weight in my new single life. I needed to figure out how to remain living
в my house and continue to make a car payment on a small salary. Honestly, I
as really struggling with the divorce, both financially and emotionally. I had
lowed myself to become emotionally dependent on my husband. Once again,
ot a proud moment.

I was suicidal during this time, thinking of more than one way to take my
fe. Of course, my parents and friends knew I wasn't myself, but I never told them
юout the negative feelings and thoughts going through my head. Then, a friend
f mine invited me to join her husband and her at a church service. I went along
nd, after that, continued to participate in going to church. This was the step I
зeded to get past the divorce and move on. Allowing God back into my life was
game-changer. That was when I realized that I needed to start carrying my own
eight again in my personal life. I made a decision: I needed a better paying job
nd to start taking care of myself again.

I had always wanted to help people by becoming a paramedic and ride an
nbulance. My ex-husband had always discouraged it, but now I went for it.
ithin months, I applied for a position with the fire department to pursue my
ream of being able to help others. I realized that I needed some serious training
» prepare for the physical ability test. Once again, I found myself doing the hard
ork that was needed to be successful. I prepared by pushing (by myself) a full-
ze pick-up truck through a church parking lot numerous times a week. I also
alled tires loaded with bags of concrete through the park. I was determined to
ass the test.

The day of the test arrived. I was extremely nervous but ready for the challenge. I remembered during the last section of the test that I needed to make an adjustment to the equipment, but the voice inside me was telling me, "Don't stop! Keep going, just do not stop!" I listened to that voice and completed the test with only one second left on the timer. The test wasn't perfect, but I was successful because I had prepared for the day.

Welcome to the Fire Department! Now I had to figure out what was required to carry my own weight daily in rookie school as a firefighter and as a paramedic. All rookies must prove themselves once they graduate and are assigned to a specific station. This is a situation where you have to pull your own weight or you might as well go and find another job. Understandably so; firefighters have to go into burning buildings when everyone else is running out, and they may need to carry someone out. Even for the guys, proving yourself as a trustworthy member of the station crew is hard. But for a female, Holy Cow! Even the general public doesn't believe that a woman can be physically strong enough for this career. The answer to proving yourself is to take things one step at a time, and always give one hundred percent effort to every task. Even the menial tasks, like mopping the floor and cleaning the toilets, you must give it your all. When a fire call comes in, you must step up and be prepared to use everything that you were taught in rookie school. On the inside, your adrenaline is pumping like crazy, but on the outside, you appear calm and collected. You have to keep moving forward and taking one step at a time, even when fear is setting in.

Over the last twenty-seven years as a firefighter and paramedic, I have experienced a lot of different situations. I reflect on each one to determine whether I pulled my own weight. I always ask myself if I could have done anything differently to affect a different, better outcome? One specific incident that I vividly remember was when a thirty-year-old male was shot multiple times by teens who were just out shooting randomly at people for no reason. The fire engine arrived on the scene first, and the man was still talking and able to communicate. My partner and I arrived in the ambulance a couple of minutes later. Now, the guy was no longer talking. He was unconscious. We placed him in the ambulance and began taking care of him. But by the time we arrived at the hospital, he had deteriorated. We performed CPR but were not able to save him. The immediate feeling I had as that I had failed. I felt I had let the man and his family down. After all, I am supposed to be the angel that comes in and makes a positive difference.

This incident replayed in my mind for days. Every time I replayed it, I knew there was nothing else I could have done. Both my partner and I had pulled our own weight. We knew what to do, how to do it, and when to do it. We were prepared for the situation. We made all the right decisions and had both given one hundred percent effort to saving the man, but we still had no control over the final outcome.

Of course, it's at times like these when we have to accept that we're only human, there's only so much you can do in some situations, and despite doing our utmost, you're going to be unsuccessful at times. I have failed and am going to fail again at times, just as we all do. But can something truly be called a failure if I give one hundred percent of myself in the attempt? Yes, I may be unsuccessful, and I get very disappointed and unhappy when things don't work out the way I want, yet I find that it is easier to accept the outcome if I know I gave it my 100%.

Stuff happens to everyone. That's life. But you have to decide if you want to be an asset or a liability. You have to ask yourself if you're going to be crippled by what happens to you, or empowered by it. I choose to be empowered! I want to carry my own weight in life and continue to get up every day and improve on my life. I realize that the real struggle is within myself, as it is within all of us, and the real battlefield is in my own mind. To achieve what I want to achieve, I must relentlessly battle against the negative thoughts, the lack of energy, the bad days that come to us all. I understand that the decisions I make in my mind every day affect my everyday actions and outcomes. Do I go to the gym today? Or do I take it easy and chill? Do I practice today? Or do I decide that it will be okay if I don't prepare?

To me, it's an incontrovertible truth that we control our own destinies through the decisions, or lack of decisions, that we make numerous times a day. All of us know this, but often we still let life make the decisions for us, and we simply go along with them, even if they're not what we really want. I believe that we must do the opposite and make the decisions that determine our lives for ourselves. Are you happy to let circumstances control you? Or do you want to control the circumstances? Life seems to me like a chain of events requiring decisions in every corner, and a wrong decision or a failure to make a decision like a weak link in that chain that can affect our whole lives.

I say, do not allow yourself to be caught up by circumstances—don't be th weak link. Instead, take some time to figure out what needs to change to mak you a stronger link—and then take the appropriate action! Keep taking one ste at a time and moving forward. Try to keep improving yourself, and always kee learning. It's up to us as individuals to decide what needs to happen to make su that we pull our own weight in our lives.

BIOGRAPHY

Toni Catchings is best known for two things: Being a strong athletic woman an her compassion to help others. She was inducted into the Sports Hall of Fame Texas A&M University-Commerce in September 2015. She continues to serv as a firefighter and paramedic. She has been promoted through the ranks ov the last twenty-seven years and currently holds the rank of Captain. She enjo helping young girls realize their true potential and to believe in themselves. To is also the owner of Catch 22 Home Solutions.

Contact Information
Facebook: http://facebook.com/toni.catchings.3
Instagram: https://www.instagram.com/monkee2022/

CHAPTER 31

CHOOSE MENTORS AND APPRECIATE FAILURES

By Tonika Bruce

I believe I was destined for greatness with a purpose to lead people. My greatest satisfaction has always come from helping people. I can look at a process and quickly suggest ways to improve it, and think of several related businesses, only to see that idea become a multi-million-dollar business within three or four years.

When 9/11 happened, I was 23-years-old. I thought it was the worst day of my life. My business seemed doomed. No one was buying or selling; people were too busy, in shock, glued to the TV. I went from making 30K a week to being afraid to buy a bag of ramen noodles. I lost everything—money, pride, and the fire within. I didn't know what to do. I had no real friends. I couldn't ask my family for help. How could I ask anyone who hadn't ever been in such a situation for help?

I credit this as my turning point—the moment when I realized that chasing money isn't the right way to do things.

I kept asking myself the same questions over and over: How did this happen to me when all I know is how to be successful? Do I see success only one way? In just one area of my life? With only certain people?

At that age, I didn't take the time to reflect on what had gone wrong; I w broke, hungry, and prideful. I thought God was angry with me. My best frien had committed suicide, and I knew how that affected me and everyone else, that was NOT an option. It seemed as if my only choices were to hustle or ju give up.

I graduated from college, enjoyed a successful career playing basketball, an was ready to continue living the so-called all-American dream. I reconnected wi the love of my life, got a great, high-end apartment, and started working until th time was right to go back to school. But even with three jobs, money was tight.

Then, I saw an ad that said $20/hour: I called the number and got a interview. I arrived early and was immediately drawn to Alan, the presente Watching him completely changed my life. I was deeply impressed by the way commanded the room and connected easily with the 50 people in the room. Th day, I felt I'd seen what success looked like—wrapped in an expensive suit, wi conviction in his voice, Alan had the ability to make people *feel* what he felt. took the job and used my rent money to purchase the required kit. It was my fir direct sales position; even with zero sales background, my competitiveness, m desire to be the best, and make a ton of money drove me from the start.

My biggest growth came from modeling Alan and reading several of th books he referenced.

Being naturally gifted and ambitious, I wanted to be the best; I advance quickly and earned the opportunity to work with the owner of the compan in Ft. Lauderdale. One of the most important lessons I learned is that havin the wrong mentor can negatively influence your chances of success if you are strong enough to fight against their effects. After a few months of working Ft. Lauderdale, I was ready to go out and open my own location in Dallas, T I prepared by attending events with people like Tony Robbins, Mark Cuba Zig Ziglar, and Les Brown. I learned that everything was possible—when I too action.

My plan was to open 300 locations in 10 years. We opened eight offices 6 months. I did interviews, hiring and training over 3000 sales representatives. the young age of 23, I was easily making a six-figure income monthly. I studie developing myself into a great speaker and teacher, even at events outside of

wn company. And then, it happened: I didn't just fall, I plummeted and landed
at on my face.

After that day, I decided it would be best if I didn't try again. I was broke—I
ad maybe $50 at best, plus credit collectors were hounding me with daily calls.
Iever in my life had I ever felt so scared, hurt, or angry, and I had no idea of what
) do to get out of the situation.

It wasn't long before that $50 became $10, which was when logic and
ecessity won out. I desperately needed money, so I got a job to fit in better with
le people around me. First off, I tried restaurant management. True, the hours
ere long, and I smelled of cooking every day, but the money was great, and I
)on became successful again. I even managed to grow our restaurant to new
vels. My time in restaurant management taught me the value of giving good
rvice, as well as humility, but soon it felt like it was the right time to leave the
.jitas behind and try something closer to my heart.

That's when I first got into basketball coaching. I had the opportunity
) watch the grind, hustle, and enthusiasm in my good friend, Dorian. He
)mmanded attention, and his intensity was infectious. Before long, his positivity
rew my thoughts back to the dreams I'd once had of greatness. My purpose
ld passion for leading, training, and developing people was leading me back to
ly roots, and my first passion—basketball. Being naturally competitive, I loved
inning, so playing for championships was always top on my list of great ways
) spend time. In a short period, I'd exchanged my expensive suit for gym shorts
ld sneakers. Okay, so the "vehicle" had changed, but so had the quality of the
lentor. That, as I was to discover, was the missing piece of the puzzle.

There's no denying that I enjoyed incredible success as a basketball coach.
ut, although I coached a team that won five championships in a single season,
 seemed as though the athletic director's sole mission in life was sabotaging my
ayers and team—just because we were successful! It was this that helped me
fficially confirm my understanding of mentors and the influence they can have
pon you. It made me realize how important it is in life to carefully choose the
eople and things you learn from. As I discovered, if you surround yourself with
ie wrong ones, your greatest accomplishments can be spoiled as a result.

It's sometimes hard to accept, I know, but trust me when I say that a ba
mentor can come in many unexpected forms; it can be a boss, the company yo
work for, a friend, co-worker, or parent. At the time, I couldn't help wonder
I was the only one who had come across a boss or a group of people apparent
dedicated to causing me to fail. I'd always believed that bosses, managers, and th
people around you are supposed to be rooting for you and helping you to succee
Clearly, I was wrong.

Then, without warning, things for me just seemed to hit a wall; I was
the top and climbing in my coaching career. I had over ten interviews and g
seven job offers, just not the three I wanted. I felt like a failure again. I felt like
was deliberately being brought low, and this time I wasn't sure I had the will
get back up.

After my grandmother passed away, I was led into a completely ne
and different field—nursing. I had gone from sales, public speaking, coachir
teenagers to wanting to care for geriatric and cardiac patients. But I wasn't su
that nursing was even worth getting excited about. Maybe this was God's way
saying that he wasn't mad at me anymore and that he was giving me another sho
One thing I was sure of, though—this was significant. It told me that my li
meant something, and whomever I was becoming, it better be good! By this tim
I'd witnessed first-hand the terrible standard of care that patients were receivir
and wanted to remedy that by being the opposite—I wanted to be THE BEST

Nursing school was absolutely exhausting! Anyone making it out alive h
rightfully earned the title WARRIOR BEAST. The small town of El Dorad
Kansas, hosts a hidden gem, one of the best nursing schools on the planet. Durir
this time, more than ever, my growth as a leader was challenged and elevate
Yes, there was a moment when I felt like quitting, when hearing the voice in n
head of my high school coach, Coach P, saying, "Finish what you start and mal
things better than you found them," just wasn't enough. My turning point can
in the third semester, when I came across an instructor named Sherry. Sherry w
super tough, which made me want to be in her clinical class. Not only was Sher
tough, but she also demanded a lot more from her students than other instructo
Under Sherry's teaching and mentorship, my previous expectations of what w

tandard" shot up the scale. She made me see that what I'd been giving and ontributing so far was simply not good enough.

In nursing school, I became president of my class for two consecutive terms n a row and formed lasting friendships with several classmates and instructors. I as honored to be the commencement speaker at our graduation ceremony. This e-ignited my fire for public speaking and encouraged me to study for my master's egree in Executive Leadership.

My quest to give my patients the best care possible was often clouded and ompromised by a lack of resources, insufficient staff, and lack of teamwork. I ook a job to be a part of something great and believed so deeply in the hiring anager's vision that I was willing to drive 90 minutes each day to reach the goal had in mind. I wanted to be a part of that success, but when both my managers ft, my motivation changed, and I found myself once again no longer positioned or success.

Arriving at a place where success was truly represented in the people round me, and finding a suitable mentor were now the most important things o me. I wanted to experience success, not just read about it on a vision board, o I continued to search for my "fit." My purpose changed from wanting to lead eople to searching for a leader to lead me in the right direction.

The day finally came when I decided that I was going to be the best leader knew and that, to achieve that goal, I had to make myself better. By chance, I ossed paths with one of the most influential leaders and mentors I have ever ome across in nursing—my then Chief Nursing Officer, Molly. Molly's motto as, "make it happen." Her smile made her look like she was having so much n, plus she had the passion that motivated her to work to elevate our team. I w success ahead of me again. This time, however, the suit was accompanied by iletto heels and flip curls. I was drawn to Molly's drive, passion, and humility. I anted to be like her.

I had a patient who'd had surgery on both eyes and couldn't see my face. attended to her in recovery, and she said I was just the person she needed to be er nurse. She asked my name, and when I said my first name only, she asked for y last name. When I told her, she smiled and said, "Ah, Dr. Bruce!" She then oceeded to tell me that I wasn't going to be just a nurse for long. I was going

to speak and lead people while heading up a successful business that would gro
internationally. She said that I might lose a few people along the way, but tha
everyone who jumped and stayed on board was going to catch that same fire tha
burned inside me. She spoke of the things I knew but never shared with anyon
The interesting part was that I had just graduated with my master's degree and ha
just been approved for doctoral admissions.

Shortly afterward, I was injured at work. The injury was severe, causin
a neuro deficit in my leg and foot. Most of the time, I couldn't feel my toes.
couldn't walk, bend over, or sit down, let alone work. As a result, my incom
plummeted from six figures to around the average household income. It seeme
to me that I'd failed again, and, this time, I was completely powerless to tak
action to change my situation. I had no choice but to be still. Initially, I wa
angry that this had happened to me, until I suddenly realized that I was actual
prepared for the situation and that, in fact, it had happened for me.

The injury slowed me down, gave me time to reflect on just how I'd arrive
at that point, what my purpose in life was, and how I could turn my situation int
a success. Looking back, I saw that I'd gone through just about every circumstan
to prepare me for this challenge.

Around this time, I was shown an opportunity involving network marketin
Without a clear plan, I accepted it and figured I had to act this time. I'd don
enough self-reflection to realize that the job I'd valued so much didn't value m
at all. I decided it was time to get back to doing things that fulfilled my purpos

Starting my own network marketing business turned out to be the be
decision I ever made in my life. I had all the necessary skills, desire, motivatio
and fire already in me to make a go of it. And, yes, that patient was correc
Some people, including family members and friends, refused to come along o
the ride. But those that did, I'm happy to say, are sharing the fruits of success rig
alongside me. For me, helping others reach their financial potential, especial
during these tough times, continues to be deeply personally rewarding. I ofte
think about that patient: She was right about my business being a success. On
day, I hope to give her a big hug and treat her to a nice lunch.

At this point in my long and sometimes challenging journey through lif
I've come to realize that no matter what my job was or how many times I faile

the past, all I needed was to see that my success had no boundaries and that, sometimes, we just need to be shown what success actually looks like.

BIOGRAPHY

Tonika Bruce is a registered nurse, speaker, change agent, and serial entrepreneur with over 20 years of experience in building businesses and teams. She is a 6-figure income earner and shares an insatiable desire for helping others find success, purpose, and prosperity. She relishes living a life of a higher purpose and is the founder of multiple non-profit organizations. Tonika strives to amalgamate her love for serving people and expertise in business to help others unlock doors to financial freedom. Tonika found success in multiple niches, including nursing, entrepreneurship, business and basketball coaching, and executive leadership.

Contact Information

Facebook: https://www.facebook.com/tonikabruce11

Instagram: http://instagram.com/tonikabruce

Website: http://tonikabruce.com

CHAPTER 32

DREAMS ARE FOR SUCKERS

By Whitney Tello

New mom. Divorced. Unemployed. I did not plan for it in my life planner. This was not the life I wanted, but this was, in fact, the life I was living. The *unimaginable* was now my *reality*. Fate played a cruel joke on me, and within eighteen months, my entire life changed its course.

Several months after my son was born, my marriage of five years began to fall apart. Soon after, things spiraled rapidly out of control and I was left with the hardest decision of my life—be a single mother or stay in an unhealthy relationship. Even though the force of habit lured me to stay, I knew it wasn't right. I was worth more. If I had stayed in that same situation, I would have settled for much less than I deserved.

I spent sleepless nights, frustrated, why could he not see my love for him? *Why could he not see what he had right in front of his face?* Such thoughts occupied my mind. He had a wife that adored him and a 'brand-new' perfectly healthy baby boy. This was supposed to be *our* time. We spent two of our five years of marriage dealing with the dreaded pains of infertility. Our son was supposed to be our beacon of light, our reward for all our pain and suffering. Little did I know, my suffering through the years of infertility was minuscule when confronted with the devastation of a broken marriage.

Imagine two people in a rowboat with stationary oars, both of them responsible for rowing their oars. But if they do not row in harmony, that boat not going anywhere anytime soon. Much like that boat, my marriage was moving in circles with no clear destination in sight. After endlessly rowing alone, my arm refused to budge. I filed for divorce. I had a surprise in store for me. Two weeks after my divorce finalized, I was let go from my job—a job in which I was recently promoted and was on track to achieve much more.

I was in the boxing ring of life, 12 rounds in and exhausted. Life was throwing all its best punches at me. I was knocked down but not yet knocked out. I had a choice: do I continue onto the 13th round, or do I give up? I could faintly hear the referee counting to 10 as my inner monologue kicked in.

"Why is this happening to me?"

"What else could go wrong?"

"This isn't fair."

"I didn't sign up for this."

"Why can't I catch a break?"

"What am I going to do?"

"You'll figure it out."

"Can he stop counting already and let me think?"

"*Get up.*"

I got up. Shaken and confused, but I carried myself into the 13th round and beyond. I realized that life takes unexpected turns. The choices of others, both indirectly and directly, affect you. Trauma and loss are intricately woven in the circle of life. At first, I focused on *why*. But those questions led me nowhere except down a rabbit hole of confusion and dismay. I was asking the wrong questions; I needed to ask *how*.

"How will I get out of this situation?"

"How will I provide for my son as a single mother?"

"How will I show my son that he has a strong and resilient mother?"

"How will I create more time and achieve financial freedom?"

"How will I ensure that my financial future is in my own hands?"

"How do I wish to be remembered?"

How will I pass on my legacy to my son if I don't start it *now*?"

Although I never desired to be an unemployed, single mother, and the circumstances were wildly out of my control, there was *one* thing that was still under my control—my actions. What I did about it was 100% my responsibility. I got up before the referee got to 10. I put my future back in my own hands. I regained control of my life and put myself in the driver's seat again.

Accepting your reality does not mean understanding your reality; there is a difference. Merely possessing knowledge doesn't produce results. People often talk about how they know what they should be doing, but they aren't doing it. So, I threw in the towel in trying to make sense of my new life. I leaned into accepting rather than understanding, and changes started to happen, slowly but surely. I made a decision that *why* no longer mattered, but *what* I am going to do about it, does.

Education doesn't prepare you for life. Only life can prepare you for life.

Are You a Sucker?

Have you ever been suckered, much like me, at a young age, to buy into the mentality that you should follow your dreams? To think that you should always believe in yourself? Or even believe that you can be anything you want to be in this world? Did you also believe that if we go to school, get into a good college, get good grades, land a good job, get married, and have kids, life would be all fine and dandy? So why is it I was a divorced, single mother, and unemployed even with a degree in business? I checked all the "right" boxes exactly how society taught me, but life still happened.

Once we transition into adults, 'dreaming big' is criticized, dismissed, rejected, and even mocked. "Aim for the stars" fades into the stern noise of "be grateful for what you have." Is it wrong to want more? Be more? Do more? It wasn't wrong for a child, then why so for an adult?

We've all heard the phrase money doesn't buy happiness. That is true. However, we also fail to mention that money does provide the means to create the lifestyle you desire for your own level of happiness. Does gardening bring you happiness? Money enables you to pay for the soil, plants, or gardening tool Does traveling with your family bring you happiness? How do you pay for the ga flights, accommodations, food, etc.?

Once I purged myself of self-sabotaging thoughts that I do not deserv more, I went for it at full speed. I have now found a life full of happiness an purpose. My mantra still rings true now as it did at the beginning of the 13t round: I don't want money to be rich, I want money to *enrich*. Yes, you can c both—have money and still enrich the lives of others.

I Will Ask Again, Are You a Sucker Too?

Have you accepted your reality? Are you ready to be in the driver's seat? You crea the life you want. You determine your future. It's up to you to bring your visic to life.

If you have a vision, do you see it clear as day? Do you live it and speak into existence? Good, then you're a sucker too. Welcome to the club! You got th vision, right? Everything in life, including your success, depends on you *protecti your vision*. You are the gatekeeper of your vision. The only person truly stoppir you from living your dream life is you.

BIOGRAPHY

Whitney Tello is a self-made entrepreneur who fought her way to the top when life knocked her down. From becoming a first-time mother to a divorcee to an unemployed single mother, Whitney was still determined to leave her mark on this world. Growing up thirty minutes outside of New York City, Whitney was accustomed to dreaming big. With a degree in Business and Spanish, and digital marketing expertise, she jumped two feet in when it came to starting a career in network marketing. Now through years of self-development and self-discovery, Whitney has made it her mission to help others get unstuck in life by sticking to their dreams and transforming them into realities. Some of her many passions include spending quality time with her son, fitness, travel, and never giving up on her lifelong quest to master the art of making the perfect pancake.

Contact Information

Facebook: https://www.facebook.com/13TeenthRound/

Instagram: https://www.instagram.com/whittywits/

Website: https://www.13teenthround.com/regain-control

THE END

Made in the USA
Middletown, DE
17 November 2020